MW01199700

Here, There, and Back Again

WANDA BLACKGRAVE

authorHOUSE®

AuthorHouse™
1663 Liberty Drive
Bloomington, IN 47403
www.authorhouse.com
Phone: 1-800-839-8640

First published by AuthorHouse 11/30/2009

ISBN: 978-1-4490-3892-2 (e)
ISBN: 978-1-4490-3890-8 (sc)
ISBN: 978-1-4490-3891-5 (hc)

Library of Congress Control Number: 2009910886

Printed in the United States of America
Bloomington, Indiana

This book is printed on acid-free paper.

Dedications

This book is dedicated to my dad, who was the best storyteller whom I have ever met. I can still hear your voice telling me that I can do anything I want in America because, "This is the land of opportunity."

I miss you!

And, also to my children in Arabia so that they may learn more about me, how much I loved them, and why I felt it best to leave Arabia. I will always love you Khalid, Nadia, and Sarah, in this life, and if I can't be with you in this life, then I will keep my faith that I will be with you in the next. We are only passing through this life for a short while. There is a part of me living in you no matter how far away you are, and no one can ever steal that away!

Verse 233

The Holy Qur-an

"The mothers shall give suck
To their offspring
For two whole years,
For him who desire
To complete the term."
" No soul shall have
A burden laid on it
Greater than it can bear."
"No mother shall be
Treated unfairly
On account of her child."

A mother in Arabia after divorce is only allowed to keep her child until the age of two and then the child is forcefully taken away by the father. Many times this is not even abided. Many babies have been taken away from mothers during the time of nursing. The court system in Saudi Arabia always rules in favor of the father even with Arabian women. An American woman is likely to be put in jail when going to court to get her children back. This has been told to me by a Saudi lawyer. Saudi Arabia is not a part of the Hague Convention which is an international agreement that requires the return of a child or children wrongly removed from a country where they belong. The American Embassy is not allowed to interfere with the laws of Saudi Arabia. This information is from much research, talking to diplomats at Embassies, and my own real life personal experiences.

Acknowledgements

My sincerest thanks to my mom, who was the first person to read my manuscript and said that it was a very good and dramatic story. If she would not have believed in me, this story may never have been told. Thanks mom, for always believing in me that I could accomplish anything if I tried. You've always been there when I needed you. Thank you, mom for helping with the editing of this book as well and to Dr. Jack Humphrey who also helped me now and in the past.

Thanks also to my sister Lisa who once said that I was the most courageous person who she has ever known. Thanks Lis for always believing in me and my writing this story. You'll always be my best friend.

Last but not least to my husband, Tim, who saved me from Arabia and always stood by me no matter what I wanted to do with my life. If it weren't for him my book may never have been published. Thanks for never giving up on me during hard times. It's all because of you.

Also thanks to my eight year old daughter, Samantha, who was a blessing from God and who has helped me to want to live and laugh once again. Her relentless energy and love for life keeps me going.

My sincere gratitude goes out to all of those who helped make my dream come true so that this book could finally be published.

Dreams can come true!

Contents

1. The Lake

*M*ost lakes seem very ordinary, unlike this particular lake which still haunts me today with it's mesmerizing scenery that I still remember. Many lazy days were spent walking with my Dad around this lake and consequently are the most memorable and happiest days of my life; for as this story unfolds, my only dream is to escape and return to this lake near my beloved hometown in Southern Indiana.

The vision of this lake is still clear in my mind as it casts an illuminating greenish blue light near the shore, with tall pine, oak, hickory, and maple trees surrounding it. A quiet rustling sound often billows from the trees as the leaves and branches sway from a cool night's breeze. Squirrels with big fluffy tails scatter under the trees spontaneously cracking hickory nuts. Numerous dark green spotted frogs silently hop near the grassy shore and nearby bank. As a light blanket of fog quickly covers the lake, the frogs begin to croak louder and louder while the sun slowly slips down through the trees. The smell of fish fills the air as a bass abruptly jumps out of the water, visible only for a second. Vast amounts of minnows flutter across the pebbles near the lake's edge. The shrill chirping of crickets permeates the lake as masses of buzzing mosquitoes hover near the lonely shore. A sweet smell emanates from the honeysuckle plants while black water moccasins eerily emerge from a secluded area and begin slithering across the murky part of the lake.

The bass were jumping out of the water tonight, so I knew Dad would catch a couple of squirming fish and sure enough as soon as he threw the purple worm-like bait in he hooked one. My dad was a great storyteller and would never stop talking until he threw the line out to catch a fish. Even then he had to whisper something in my ear which was either a joke or something about how to catch a fish. He didn't like it when I threw rocks in the water, but he was the one who taught me how to make skinny flat rocks skip across the lake. When I was bored it was fun, but he said that it scared all the fish away.

As a child, I always wondered what was on the other side of this murky, enchanting lake. Could there be something mysterious maybe even fascinating over there; or, were there strange nocturnal creatures lurking around through the fog that I didn't need to know about? Since I was only five years old, wandering off alone into those dark, endless woods didn't seem very wise at the time.

Little did I know that someday I would be going to the other side, but it would be the other side of the world.

I asked Dad many times if we could go to the other side of the lake to fish, and he said that this side of the lake was better for fishing. He told me that it's not always "better on the other side," and that I would probably find that out someday.

As the sun is slowly dispersing over the serene lake, I follow my Dad through the tall prickly weeds with our mischievous black, brown and white spotted beagle Frisky, naturally tagging along and sniffing everything along the way. I vividly remember the peaceful feeling I had while fishing with my dad, but I never knew those moments would follow me wherever I unknowingly went to the other side of the world.

As a teenager I vicariously imagined from movies and books what the Middle East would be like. Omar Sharif was so mysteriously dark and handsome. I wondered what life would be like being married to a foreigner. It might be interesting to travel where so much biblical history had occurred. I thought that maybe it would help me learn more about God by learning about a different people and their religion. Sometimes I pondered what it would be like to be married to an Arab, completely knowing this would be utterly impossible living in such a small Southern Indiana town. Strangely enough, I ended up marrying an Arab.

After graduating from high school, I enrolled in an airline academy in St. Louis, Missouri. I decided that I wanted to be a flight attendant, but my highly educated mom felt that it was best that I had some computer training as well. I reluctantly studied to be a reservationist. The first day of class I met Heidi whose complexion was very fair. I told her she was as white as the moon. She was from Fairbanks, Alaska. She said that they don't get much daylight so lying out in the sun there was out of the question.

The first time we went to the pool at our apartment complex, her face and her body became as red as a beet. I couldn't stop laughing, even though I knew she was in pain. I told her she would have to put some aloe on for a week or so. We became good friends, and I still would like to go to Alaska to find her to see how she's doing. To this day I wish that I would have waited for Alaskan Airlines to come to our school, but this was not my destiny. They were the last well known airline that was coming to look for employees, so Heidi had to wait the longest to be hired. I was full of energy and too impatient to wait for three months for Alaskan Airlines. Continental Airlines was a very popular airline at the time, so I decided to interview with Continental and was one of the first students hired. Why I chose to live in Houston, Texas is beyond me considering all the other places I could have gone.

Is it fate why things happen or could it be that the lives that we lead have already been planned for us before we were even born; thus, we can't change what happens to us no matter how hard we try? Numerous Arabic women told me that our lives have already been planned for us by God, just like a movie. The Arabs have a saying that what was written for our lives cannot be changed because it was written by God as soon as we have a soul. The Arabs also say when it is your time to die no one can prevent that hour from coming because that exact time and place was written by God.

One good example of this is when I watched the movie "Lawrence of Arabia". Lawrence and a tribe of Arabs were crossing the desert when one man couldn't keep up with the rest of the tribe. When a few men noticed he was missing, it was too far for anyone to travel back to find him since their supply of water was so low. The Arab leader of the tribe said that it was written that it is his time to die. However, Lawrence believed that he could change things and the way the Arabs believed. He went back into the desert through a sandstorm and found the man barely alive. Lawrence put him on his camel to carry him back to the tribe. The tribe was shocked that Lawrence had come back alive with this man. The man did survive, but not for long because by nightfall this same man had gotten in a fight with an Arab from another tribe. The Arab law says that any man who kills someone must be shot or beheaded. Lawrence heard about this and said that he would take care of the situation since he was an outsider who could keep these tribes from fighting about who would punish this man. Lawrence fearlessly walked toward the man who was kneeling in the sand with his head facing downward. Lawrence told the man to raise his head. As the man slowly raised his head Lawrence saw who he was and despair overtook him. It was the same man whose life he had saved in the desert. Astonished by who he saw, Lawrence stumbled backward then asked the man if he had willingly killed another man. The man's reply was yes. Lawrence told him to get up off his knees and then shot him. The leader of the Arab tribe said again that it was written. It was written by God for this man to die on this day and no one, not even Lawrence of Arabia could prevent it.

*I'm the youngest, with Frisky my beagle, Mom, Dad,
and my sisters in the backyard next to the lake.*

2. How We Met

I met Mubarak when I was working for Continental Airlines in Houston, Texas. I was nineteen at the time and working as a reservationist. His friend was actually the one making a reservation. My mundane life was about to change forever when this very charismatic man with a heavy accent called to make a reservation. He asked me to go out with him. I said no that I didn't want to, but he was very persistent and gave me his name and number. He told me to think about it, but if I didn't want to call him to just throw his number away. His name was Abraham, and my guess was that he might have been a foreigner. Strangely enough, I did like his charming accent. After ending his call, the calls from other patrons were coming in like crazy which is the advantage of working with a huge airline- no breaks whatsoever. As I started making another reservation, I nonchalantly threw his telephone number in the small trash can that was squished under my desk. I really wasn't in the mood to meet a stranger that day.

Yet, at the end of the day, for some strange reason, I took the paper out of the trash and put it in my overly stuffed purse, not realizing it was the biggest mistake of my life. I thought maybe I would change my mind later, like I often did, and would call him.

That night I did change my mind and called the number to say hi to this foreign sounding man, but his friend Mubarak answered the phone instead. I liked to hear his voice with that heavy enticing accent. He asked me if I wanted to go for dinner, and we could meet his friend later, who he said was an airplane pilot. I said okay, and we went out to eat at an authentic Arabian restaurant. I never did meet his friend, Abraham, until much later. It seemed strange that he just took his friend's date away and never uttered a word about Abraham.

Mubarak was very easy going and mysteriously handsome with his black somewhat thick curly hair, honey brown eyes, a moustache, and beautiful olive skin. He stood about five foot six. He did surprisingly look a bit like Omar Sharif. The night we went out he was wearing a nice pair of black dress pants and a fancy shirt. I noticed that he always dressed very nicely and was always shaved.

His name was hard for me to pronounce at first so I called him Mike. He was always smiling and never seemed to let anything bother him. I told him that I could help him improve his English because I didn't understand what he was saying half the time.

During those first months, I don't remember him ever being very controlling as he would soon become as time went on. He would call me his habeebatee. That means "my love" in Arabic.

He was very generous and would buy me expensive clothes or anything that I wanted including gold, which I had never thought of buying before. He said that I had to wear gold. All the women wear gold where he came from. He bought me a long white fluffy fur coat that cost over a thousand dollars which I still have but hardly ever wear it if at all. He said that nothing was too good for me.

At the time he was studying English at the University of Houston. He told me that he didn't want to continue with his studies. He talked about going home to help manage a factory that his dad owned. I thought that was great that his dad owned a factory and was doing so well financially. That must be how he was able to live here and go to school.

While I was working for Continental Airlines I would visit him, but the late nights that he was used to were tiresome for me having to get up and go to work at seven in the morning. Holidays of course were big workdays as well, so I had to work on the Fourth of July, but Mubarak didn't seem to mind. He just liked going out late at night anyway. Many nights we were out until three or four, especially during the month of Ramadan which is the month of fasting for all Muslims. The Muslims that I met liked to stay up all night and sleep until noon during the month of Ramadan. Mubarak said it was a special time for all Muslims.

I noticed that he always used a credit card to buy most of our groceries and anything else that was needed. It never occurred to me that those credit cards weren't really his from the way he talked. I thought that his dad must have helped him get his own credit card or anything else that he needed.

He took me to many fancy Arabian and Indian restaurants to introduce me to the food of his ethnicity. The food was really good and spicy to say the least, and in addition, we both enjoyed each other's company. He liked Indian food because his mom used to cook it. She lived in India when she was younger.

We both enjoyed dancing at some of the biggest nightclubs in Houston. I should have noticed his possessiveness showing through after he broke an ashtray on another man's head on the dance floor one night. He said that he didn't like that man staring at me. He suddenly grabbed my hand and told me to run because we needed to get out of there. I often wonder if that man that he attacked was all right because as we were leaving, I saw people crowding around the dance floor, and I noticed there was blood gushing out of the man's head. I sure hoped that he was not hurt badly. I stopped dead at the door after I saw the blood on the man's head. I wanted to help him and started walking back toward the dance floor, but before I could take another step Mubarak had picked me up and was carrying me outside to the car. I told Mike that he shouldn't do things like that in public, and that there were other ways to deal with situations besides violence. He said that the other man started the fight and tried to hit him first. I decided I'd better let it go at that.

We went to a different nightclub almost every night. Some of the Arabian nightclubs had belly dancers. The girls were beautifully shaped with hair that hung down to their hips. The costumes that they wore were embellished with silver, blue and gold sequins. Their dresses were made of satin greens and blues. It looked like great exercise to belly dance, and their outfits were unbelievably gorgeous.

One day he told me to quit my job and marry him. He said that as much money as he had, I didn't need to work and that he would take care of me, and we would eventually move back to his country. It must have been the mystique of it all. He was so different in his ways then anybody I had ever met. Little knowing how drastically this man would change my life, we eloped after a brief two month's courtship.

As we were walking to our apartment one day, he told me not to step on any ants because God would be mad. Mubarak said the ants will talk in the afterlife. He said the ants hear everything we say and feel. I couldn't believe somebody could talk me into not stepping on an ant. I started laughing and wondered if they really could hear me or know my thoughts and what about all of those ants that I had killed when I was younger? This was ridiculous. I had to stop looking at ants for awhile.

When I looked into his dark eyes he seemed so sincere and truthful about everything. Little did I know that lies were a normal part of life for him. He lied to me the entire time we were living in Houston. Later on, when it was too late, I found out that he was paying his entire bills with stolen credit cards.

After being married for three months he decided that he wanted to go back home to Saudi Arabia. He said that we could go to Indiana so I could tell my parents that I was going to the Middle East to live with this Arabian man. I don't remember my parents saying much, but my dad looked at me and said, "Are you sure this is what you want to do?" I said that I knew Mubarak wasn't an American, but he was really good to me (or so I thought), and I loved him. I was going to go to the Middle East with my husband no matter what anybody said. My dad shook his head and said that I wouldn't be back for a long time. I knew that, but I definitely wasn't thinking about the future at the time or what the Middle East was like. I was curious about what life was like on the other side of the world.

We stayed at my parent's house on Christmas Eve, and my mom was making a cake. I asked her why in the world she was making a homemade birthday cake on Christmas Eve. She said that Mubarak told her that Christmas Eve was his birthday. I remarked that he didn't tell me that. I went to ask him, and he said that he was truly born on Christmas Eve. I was appalled that he hadn't told me. After we had our Christmas dinner, we sang happy birthday to Mubarak, and he blew out the candles and ate his homemade chocolate birthday cake. I gave him a kiss and told him happy birthday.

Later on when I was living in the Middle East, I found his birth certificate that was printed in English. He was born in Doha, Qatar on September 13. His mother confirmed to me that the certificate was correct. I pondered on this for awhile. I was very angry at first for him lying to my mom. How could I ever explain to her that my husband lied and his birthday wasn't on Christmas Eve? Was this some kind of sick game? I remember asking his mom why he did this to my mom. She just laughed and said hywon (that means animal in Arabic). She just said that he was an animal and never said anything else. I had a hard time trusting him after that. My parents were so hospitable to him, and he had lied to them. This wouldn't be the first time.

3. Yemen

We left Indiana after a week to travel to the Middle East to meet his family who were living in Saudi Arabia. But first, we had to go to Sanaa, Yemen, wherever in the world that was. I had no idea, but I was going to find out and soon. Mike said that Sanaa was one of the oldest cities in the world, dating back to the 6th Century B.C., and that Noah's son Shem settled there with his family after the great flood as recorded in the Bible. Yemen is close to where the beginning of the world had started, so Mubarak told me. The Queen of Sheba lived here as well, and there is a hotel in Yemen named after her.

I have done some research from that time and found out that he was right about the history of Yemen. It is shown on a map that Yemen is south of Saudi Arabia by the Gulf of Aden and the Arabian Sea and to the west of the Red Sea. The reason that we had to go to there first was because I didn't have a visa to get into Saudi Arabia nor did Mubarak.

The flight to Yemen was extremely long, and made me wonder if I was doing the right thing traveling to a Middle Eastern country basically with a strange man, and I'm sure my family thought that I had completely "lost it."

I always wondered why I was such a stubborn person and never wanted to listen to my mom, which often caused me to wind up in trouble. Now I was going to Yemen, which could have been on another planet as I had no clue where I was going.

It took almost two days to get there because of the air flight layovers. Jordon was the country of the first layover causing us to wait in the airport most of the day. Some of the women were wearing short plaid skirts with long black boots and had their hair covered with very colorful scarves. Although I didn't realize it at the time, there was more freedom in this country than Saudi Arabia or Yemen. The language was my biggest concern because I didn't know Arabic, and it was by far the most unusual language that I had ever heard. I didn't feel comfortable when Mubarak (I had to call him Mubarak now instead of Mike) was talking to so many strange people, and I had no idea what they were saying. The further we got away from the United Stated the less English I was hearing and the more homesick I felt.

When we finally arrived in Yemen, Mubarak told me that I would have to start covering myself. Mubarak informed me that all women Muslim or not were required to cover themselves from head to toe with a huge, black cape, called an abiyah. (with a long i) This garb was required when women appeared in public but not in their own homes. This was the law.

I was so relieved to get off that plane when suddenly I had a queasy kind of feeling in my stomach. It was like the feeling right before you take an important test. I guess this was what they say is culture shock.

As people were leaving the airport through the exit doors, sand would blow in as the doors were left slightly open. As I walked out of the dusty glass doors of the airport into my new strange world, the sand immediately attacked my eyes. There was a sandstorm stirring up which would definitely take some getting used to. It seemed impossible to keep the sand from blowing into my eyes. It didn't help wearing contacts which caused my eyes to tear. My eyes slowly adjusted to the squinting, and there in the distance I saw a huge, shiny, marbled, mosque that looked like the Taj Mahal. It was indescribable and looked like a castle! Of course at that time I didn't know anything about mosques and very little about Islam. In 1985 there wasn't much talk about the Middle East in the little town that I came from. Now after doing some research I found that this was one of the biggest mosques in the world.

Suddenly, there was this mysterious, sad sound, as though somebody was ill or dying. Mubarak replied that the priest was calling people to come pray for the afternoon prayer. Muslims were to pray five times a day. This prayer call is called the "athan" in Arabic. I found myself dumbfounded! Their religion didn't even really cross my mind until now when I saw the mosque and heard the call to prayer. Scary thoughts were racing through my mind as I realized the freedom that I enjoyed in my country was gone. My country was so far away, and I was just feeling very naïve and frightened about everything that was happening to me.

The sandstorm was picking up. It was getting harder to see, and the sand was pushing its way into my mouth now. The taste of dirt was evident. It reminded me of the times when I was at the beach and sand would inevitably end up in my mouth. The road was quickly becoming covered with sand and blowing just like powdered snow blows across the roads, but this wasn't beautiful like snow.

It was clear that we needed a taxi because Mubarak's friends weren't at the airport to pick us up. The Arabic men standing on the sidewalk were staring at me and mumbling something to Mubarak. Mubarak looked distraught to say the least. I asked what the men were talking about. Mubarak said, "They are saying it's a sin that you're not covered." I said, "I'm an American and I'm not a Muslim so why should I have to cover myself?" Mubarak said, "Because this is our way." "It is the law of Islam."

It was unreal how the men looked, just like they came straight out of the Bible. They wore long white dresses with white turbans on their heads, and they wore black or brown sandals. Sand was clinging to their feet just like after a day at the beach. It was amazing how their white dresses looked so clean with all the dust and sand blowing.

Mubarak suddenly motioned for an old dirty white taxi and told me to get in the backseat while he sat in front with the driver. We were going to his friend's house that was in the city of Sanaa. The backseat of the taxi was covered with a blanket of white sheep fur that was lined with huge green beads. The car smelled musty. It seemed too warm to be sitting on thick sheep fur. The taxi driver had a dark complexion with black hair. He wasn't shaved and looked as though he needed a hot shower. All the men looked like they just had a great tan to me because it was an olive colored skin tone. I was wishing that I wasn't so white. I was getting the feeling that I really stood out. It took about thirty minutes to get to the city. As I was trying to absorb as much as

I could in my new environment I felt like I was in never, never land. I was waiting for Tinker Bell to fly over my head.

As we drove away from the airport, all I saw for miles was desert and brown barren mountains surrounding the entire area. Mubarak said that the Yemeni's chose this area because during war times it was too hard for the enemy to cross over the mountains.

I didn't see any women as we drove down the road. Of course it was an amazing sight to see packs of huge camels galloping freely through the serene desert. They made me laugh as their heads were bobbing around as they ran. Camels walk proudly, but they don't look very coordinated as they run. It looked extremely odd as well as dangerous because they were getting so close to the highway we were traveling. There weren't any barriers to keep the camels off the road so the taxi driver would slow down if he saw them starting to cross the road. The barren desert went on for miles and miles. There wasn't a tree in sight and the sand was continuously blowing over the road. For some reason I was thinking that I would never see the beautiful snow again since I would now be living in a desert. I was already missing my country.

When we reached the city, the women in the street were wearing long flowing black capes, black veils, and black gloves. Some women had their eyes visible through two small holes in the veil. It was eerie not seeing their faces. I kept wondering what they looked like. "They are supposed to walk behind their husbands," Mubarak quietly murmured.

The buildings were made of a light colored stone and so ancient beyond the place of where I came from. I saw a picture of a chicken on a sign, on top of a roof and surmised it was a restaurant that served chicken. Mubarak said that it was something like our Kentucky Fried Chicken, but the men were only allowed inside to eat. There were no women allowed. I said, "Well, that's not fair." "What if I decide to just walk in?" He said, "They won't let you in, so don't even think about it!"

As we continued driving there were sheep crossing the road causing the driver to frequently stop the car. Seeing sheep crossing the road and camels running around loose seemed very weird to me. Everybody was honking their horns at the sheep and each other, which was a normal phenomenon according to the taxi driver. I didn't see any stop signs or lights so I guess that's why they had to honk and yell at each other. It was total chaos! People crossing the street looked as though they were risking their lives. The drivers seemed very angry when they had to stop to let a pedestrian pass. Some men trying to cross the street would bang on the hood of the cars and would yell at the driver as they were crossing the road. I then noticed that many drivers were yelling at a sheepherder and told him to hurry up and get his stupid sheep across the road. Mubarak was telling me what they were saying in English. They would just laugh as they were yelling and honking. It seemed as though they were deliberately trying to hit the people crossing the road. The drivers would slightly bump into the people and the sheep. It all seemed so primitive. I remember my Uncle Keith telling me about this. He was in the navy approximately fifty years ago and made a stop in Yemen. He said he saw the same thing. Things must never change here. I don't know if that's a good thing or a bad thing. I was thinking that they must be beyond stubborn to not want to change their ways and make some improvements.

We traveled on a rocky dirt road before finally arriving at the house where we were going to stay for awhile or until I could get a visa to get into Saudi Arabia.

Mubarak's friend happily greeted us, and I was led by two smiling women to a separate room. I could smell incense burning somewhere as I walked through the house, but it was giving off a strange scent. It smelled similar to the incense one would smell in the Catholic Church for a holiday mass. I presumed it must have been frankincense or myrrh. Mubarak told me later that it was. Incense was usually lit on Fridays which was like our Sabbath which is on Sundays or the day of rest. Although, Mubarak told me once that God doesn't need a day to rest because he is God, and God doesn't get tired. It did seem to make sense, but I gave up after awhile arguing on that one. Everybody has their own religious beliefs, and who am I to know what's right or wrong.

I glanced at the long dresses that the women were wearing that went all the way down to their feet. I actually couldn't see their feet. I thought if I had to wear a long skirt like that I would trip over myself as flighty as I am. Their hair was covered with black scarves; however, some strands of black hair were visible on their forehead. The women had beautiful olive colored skin. The suntan look that I wished I had.

Obviously, I didn't know them and couldn't understand what they were saying. Two took me to a bedroom that included one single bed with a dark brown dresser. It was a small room but seemed cozy. An older woman with large honey brown eyes brought me a white scarf to cover my head because I had to keep my head covered from now on so that the men couldn't see my hair as I walked through the house. I wondered why I had to wear a white scarf, and they were wearing black. This entire situation was getting more and more strange. The older woman left and a younger pretty woman with olive colored skin smiled and motioned me to lie down. After two days without sleep, I wasn't in the mood to argue, and I didn't know her language to argue or complain anyway, so I laid down to take a nap. When I awoke, the room was completely dark and the house was very quiet, then I heard that strange sound from the mosque again. It was the prayer call. Such a sad, eerie, yet peaceful sound it was. It gave me the chills. I wondered where Mubarak was, so I anxiously opened the door and walked out.

I saw two young girls with very long black hair and an older woman sitting on the floor watching television in what appeared to be their living room. There weren't any couches or furniture, just carpet to sit on. The television was very small, and it was setting on a small table. I sat down and watched television with them and eagerly tried to communicate using facial expressions. Obviously, my communication with them was very limited so then and there I decided that I had better learn Arabic.

The days lingered on as I lived with this hospitable Arabian family, in the meantime, I learned some of their customs, as well as what food they ate and tried to understand why they stayed separated from the men. Their husbands, brothers or any other immediate family, were allowed to see them but absolutely no strange men. Muslims had to do what the Prophet Muhammad did and said which was called a Hadith. However, there was an old woman who sat with us one time. I asked Mubarak why she was allowed to sit here with her hair uncovered- not wearing a black scarf- while he was in the room. He said that she was older, so it didn't really matter. That was one of the first times that I noticed some inconsistencies with Islam.

One night Mubarak brought me a notebook that I used to write down translations. I would write as many words as I could in English as Mubarak told me the Arabic word. He would teach me a few new words everyday.

One of the first words that I learned was tea because they drank that five to six times a day. That's "shohee" in Arabic-with a short o. They put loads and loads of sugar in their hot tea, and it kept me hyper all day-that was for sure. Sometimes in the morning for breakfast they would add milk to the tea along with some ginger. The ginger made it spicy which made it a soothing warm drink in the winter. One day I told Mubarak that I didn't want to drink hot tea, and I was dying for some iced tea. He said that it would be an insult to the women if I didn't drink or eat their food. I wondered at that point if they even used ice or knew what it was because I never saw anybody have a drink with ice in it. You would think living in a hundred and twenty-five degree desert that somebody would want ice water. Anyway, out of respect I always tried to take a sip of whatever drink they made or food they had.

The food, mostly the lamb, tasted a bit unusual to me, and at this time I would have given up anything just for a plain old hamburger. Breakfast consisted of black olives, feta cheese, jam, boiled eggs, and pita bread. It was a good thing that I liked black olives because they ate a lot of them, but I don't remember ever eating them for breakfast. It reminded me of home when my sisters and I were little and mom would open a can of black olives. We would put them on our finger-tips and eat them one by one. She gave us that "mom" look. Then we all laughed and she joined our black olive eating venture. I was getting homesick again....

Their main meal was at lunch that took place around two o'clock. This was usually mutton, lamb, or chicken. The women made their own bread and chopped a huge piece of lamb with an ax to cut it into smaller pieces. The Arabic kitchen was in a small open room outside the house. It looked like a little hut, but it was made with huge concrete blocks. I didn't see a door made for it. It was very cold in January trying to cook a warm meal outside-that was for sure. They wore only sweaters as they worked to prepare the meal. I was glad that I had brought a few sweaters with me. I had no idea it could get so cold in the mornings during the winter. It felt cold enough to snow.

The women made something called molokeeya which was something like spinach, but slimy like seaweed. It was made with chicken, some garlic and onions, resembling stew and was eaten over white rice. Lemon was squeezed on the top and olive oil was poured over the top as well. Surprisingly, this became one of my favorite dishes. I always called the green stuff seaweed because it was so slimy, and it looked exactly like the seaweed floating along the shores at the beach. Mubarak never did tell me the name of it in English. I'm sure he probably didn't know. Later on I found out that it was Egyptian Spinach.

After lunch almost everybody except some of the younger overly energetic children took a nap and then at five or so the men would leave for work again. The children finished school at one-thirty everyday Saturday through Wednesday. I thought they were lucky to have gotten off school so early, but found out that the schools here started promptly at seven with no lunch being served at the school. They came home to eat which worked out well since the mothers and fathers and whole families were home at this time. It was a very family oriented culture.

The evening meal was served at eight thirty or nine o'clock at night. This was somewhat like breakfast. There was cheese, honey, jelly, labnah, (cream and cheese dip) hummus, pita bread, a meat or chicken sauce for dipping, and eggs fried with tomatoes. It didn't surprise me that the women were good cooks because for one thing there wasn't much else for them to do but cook and take care of all their children. They weren't allowed to work outside of the home. Since families were large for the most part, they were very busy taking care of the house and children and seemed generally happy.

I noticed right away that the women were very friendly and had a good sense of humor. They never left the house much when I was there; still, they seemed content with their lives. Staying in the house most of the time made me stir crazy, and I was relieved one day when Mubarak finally told me that he would take me to the city in Sanaa, Yemen. He bought me an abiyah (a black cape), a black scarf, and a burgha that is a veil to cover my face. He took me to some shops in the city that were called "souks" in Arabic. There was gold being sold everywhere, and it didn't look like the gold that we had in America. This was the shiniest most beautiful glittering gold that I had ever seen- just like in the movies. There were many different kinds of hand made jewelry, and there was material of all kinds of mesmerizing colors that was imported from Egypt and India.

We kept walking and went inside what was sort of a barn. I saw hay spread out all over the ground and in a corner there was a tan colored, grumpy looking camel lying down in a tent, and of course I wanted to get up close to it. Its eyes and lips were huge. Unexpectedly, an older man with long white hair and a long white beard walked toward me and put a big sugar cube in my hand to give to the camel and almost simultaneously, it got up and spit at me. I had no idea that they could spit so far, belch so loud, and be so grouchy and noisy. I did get up enough nerve to climb up on it and take a ride which, believe me, was nothing like being on a horse. It was a really high, bumpy ride, and I just wanted to get off because this camel was very grouchy for some reason that day. It kept spitting, grunting, and making faces as well as showing its huge teeth. I was hoping that I didn't have to ride on one of these across the desert anytime soon like Lawrence of Arabia had done.

After my enlightening experience with the camel, we walked down a very old and decrepit looking street and got something to eat. There were Schwarma's which was lamb or chicken mixed with a salad, spread with a mayonnaise kind of sauce, and wrapped in pita bread. I must admit that the food was awesome, most of the time, but it took me awhile to get used to eating lamb and getting used to new spices. They used a lot of parsley in all their foods and spices that included cinnamon, curry, turmeric, allspice, and cloves. These were a few spices that I noticed. They didn't eat much or any beef at all. They weren't allowed to eat pork because pigs were dirty and caused diseases. It was against Islam to eat pork and if you did, you were called a capher which is an Atheist in English. A person could be punished for eating pork or go to hell. I never did hear what the punishment was, but I loved pork and missed it terribly. I decided that as soon as I got a chance to visit my parents again that I would have them make me some pork chops, but of course I didn't utter a word to Mubarak about how I missed eating pork and especially bacon. There wasn't any bacon to be found in Yemen.

As we walked down the street, I grabbed Mubarak's hand, but he said that we weren't allowed to hold hands in public in this country because the police would arrest us. I also had to keep myself covered from now on so the police would leave us alone. I found it hard to believe that we could never hold hands or have any kind of personal contact in public again. That was sad to say the least because when we were in Houston, we held hands as soon as we walked out the door. I often wondered why the men were allowed to walk down the street holding hands, but a husband and wife weren't allowed this type of physical contact. Mubarak did tell me though that if two men were caught being together they would be beheaded.

Mubarak never really did talk too much about his religion in the beginning. He said that I would slowly learn that the Islamic religion was what governed the citizens. The people also lived their lives based on the traditions of the Prophet Muhammad. I asked Mubarak if the prophet Muhammad married a young girl. Mubarak said that he did marry a girl that was nine years old. So that's why I was meeting girls that were only eleven, twelve, or thirteen and married. They were so young to be thrown into a marriage.

Sanaa, Yemen; a castle in the background and houses made of stone.

4. The Princess and the Gold

I remember going to visit a friend of Mubarak's in Sanaa, Yemen. We were going to spend a night or two at his house that was further out into the country. When we arrived it looked like a castle with so many huge rooms. We went with another couple. The man was Yemeni, and his wife was from Rumania. Her name was Loomee. She could speak English fairly well so it was nice to have a friend to communicate with. She could also understand some Arabic. Mubarak's friend led us upstairs to a huge living room. The room had the longest Persian rug that I had ever seen. There were beautiful silk cushions surrounding the room. The mixture of reds, yellow, blue, and green colors were striking. As I heard the men talking my guess was he was of Yemeni royalty, and Mubarak then told me that he was. I don't recall his name, and he didn't stay to talk with us. He said that he had business to attend to, but we could stay as many days as we liked, and then he left the room. I felt awkward staying in this strange man's castle. Mubarak and his friend ordered their sheesha and bong so they could smoke, and to this day I don't know what they were smoking. I guessed it was some kind of drug because it always mellowed Mubarak and made his left eye float around. I was thankful when Loomee wanted to go exploring and look for the princess, so I didn't have to smell the smoke coming out of that bong. For some reason I just didn't care for that type of smell. I didn't know that he had a wife. Why didn't she come out to say hi? Loomee said that she had talked to one of the maids upon entering the house that had told her about the princess. She told me to follow her, and we would find the princess. As we walked through this huge marbled hallway, we passed many beautifully decorated rooms. Then Loomee stopped at a small room where a maid was standing by the door. Loomee asked if we could go in, and the maid said that she would ask the princess if it would be okay. She suddenly motioned us to go in. I wondered why a princess was sitting in this small room with all those other huge beautiful empty rooms around. We walked in, and she nodded at us and motioned us to sit down. The maid brought us some shahee (tea) and cake. The princess was a beautiful young girl. She was covered with gold jewelry. There was a gold band around her head. She also wore a belt made of solid gold. She was wearing earrings, necklaces, and many bracelets all made of the most sparkling gold I have ever seen. She was basically covered in gold from head to foot. She looked no older than eleven or twelve. Of course Loomee asked her in Arabic how old she was and confirmed that I was right about her age. I wanted to know why she was sitting here all alone, and Loomee asked her in Arabic. She said that she liked this room and would sit here until her husband called on her. We asked if her husband was nice to her. She said that she had just gotten married and that he was an older man. She smiled and said that he was kind to her. I asked the princess if she could go sit with us. Loomee translated in English to me that she couldn't because she wasn't allowed to sit with any strange men. She was also told to stay in her room. We didn't stay too long because she seemed a bit tired. She was very nice but didn't seem to be in the mood to talk very much, so we bid her a goodnight. It was around midnight. I told Loomee it must be way past her bedtime as young as she was. We headed down the hallway, but Loomee still wanted to wander around. I told her that we shouldn't go snooping around in somebody else's house, especially a castle. There must have been thirty or more rooms in this place. What a great place for kids to run around and play hide- and- seek or maybe to hide from your husband when he becomes annoying. I was daydreaming and jumped when Loomee said that she was hungry. About then we somehow stumbled into an enormous kitchen where some Phillipino maids were making a late dinner, presumably for us. Loomee took a few olives for a snack before we headed back to our room. It was Ramadan, so it was normal to have a big dinner at midnight. Shortly after, we got back to the living room where our husbands were sitting; dinner was then served by two maids. We had lamb and rice with every fruit that I could think of and other appetizers as well. I thought that the man of this castle was very hospitable to have his maids cook for us while he wasn't even there. The next morning the prince, or whoever he was, returned and Mubarak and his friend went to talk with him. Later on Mubarak told me that he was the one who helped to get my exit visa from Yemen and an entry visa for Riyadh, Saudi Arabia. I guess it's good to be friends with a prince so you can get the help you need.

5. The First House

A full month had passed before we moved into an apartment. Mubarak was seldom there so I spent most of the time alone. I would look out the window and watch the young girls walking home from school wearing their abiyahs (black capes) with their faces covered. I used to laugh and think that they looked like they were getting ready to go out trick or treating. I told Mubarak that it looked like they were having Halloween everyday, and he said that was their beliefs and ways to keep the women completely covered. He said that it was the Hadith of the Prophet Muhammad and that all Muslims were to do as the prophet said and did. Mubarak said that it kept women safe from any strange men looking at them and was supposed to help prevent divorce, rape, or other type of disgrace to happen.

Mubarak left every morning and didn't come back until eight or nine at night. He brought me the Holy Qur'an and some other books about Islam. He told me to read them, and I would find out everything that I wanted to know in the Qur'an. I loved to read and was eager to learn why the Muslims acted the way they did, so I read my new books everyday and taught myself the Arabic alphabet.

One morning while I was reading the Qur'an, there was an indescribable sound coming from the villa below. It was sad, beautiful, and eerie all at the same time almost like the sounds that came from the mosque when it was time for prayer. A young boy was reading the Qur'an aloud. He read it very loud, and I heard a donkey below that kept hee-hawing at the same time. I wondered why there was a donkey outside on the neighbor's patio. There seemed to be a lot of donkeys that lived close by and that were allowed to roam around on the roads. The sounds combined together basically just gave me the chills, and I needed to get out of this apartment and take a walk even though Mubarak told me not to go out and walk because I could be kidnapped, especially since I was an American.

The bars around the windows and the balcony weren't much help to keeping any kind of sanity. I wondered if the men who built the houses and apartments were told to put bars to further alienate the women or was it protection from thieves or intruders.

In a few weeks we moved into a house about ten minutes from the city. As we drove down the sandy rock covered street to the house, I saw what looked like a pack of big black dogs. There must have been twenty or thirty in just this one area. I had my window rolled down and could hear them growling at each other as they were fighting. I winced as I saw that a pack of them was chewing on a dog that must have lost the fight. Mubarak said they were wild dogs and acted like wolves. There went my plan for taking a healthy walk down the street. The dirty street also covered with trash was abandoned except for the dogs. I wondered where the children played. Hopefully, they weren't allowed to come out into these streets.

There were huge rectangular gray stone walls around every house. The stone walls surrounding me and the aqua sky above was all I could see. Of course the huge brown mountains could be seen in the distance, but it was rather dull to look at after awhile since it was without any greenery whatsoever. Our house was also surrounded with stone brick walls like the other houses which were at least thirty feet high. When looking out the barred up windows all that could be seen was the stone gray wall. It was scary as though I was being locked in a jail. There was a big steel door to go through to get inside the yard of the house. It could be bolted with a huge bar from the inside. This was the same for the house as well. The yard wasn't really a yard to me because it was covered with dirt and big white rocks with a few cactus plants here and there.

The inside of the house was creepy maybe because it felt so cool and was dark. This seemed odd that the house was cool being in a desert. The 60 watt bulbs that hung from the ceiling didn't help much.

There were three fairly big rooms, one bathroom, and a large kitchen. There wasn't any carpet. The floor was bare concrete. I was glad to see that there was a bed with a dresser, but they didn't have built in closets. The clothes were put in a cabinet which included drawers and a place to hang clothes.

Something that always bothered me about the houses in Yemen or Saudi Arabia was not having any closets. I never did find out why people didn't build closets in their houses for storage. Evidently they didn't know what built in closets were or didn't care to find out.

There were some hospitable Lebanese men that shared the house with us. They lived in another part of the house, so we really didn't see them much. Interestingly, they were marvelous cooks. As I recall, I loved their grape leaves stuffed with meat and rice. It was called warg-al aynub. I could have eaten it all the time. They would cook every night when they got home from work and many times would send me some food. I would do the same when I cooked. I didn't realize that I was learning the Arabic custom already. The Arabs enjoyed trading things.

The Lebanese language sounded different when they spoke Arabic to Mubarak. I found that every Arabic country and its people had different dialects and different ways of speaking that confused me even more in my efforts to learn this very difficult and harsh language. I was already learning that they read from right to left which was extremely confusing.

Unfortunately, since we moved into the new house there were new creatures coming out of hiding. These were the yellow and very deadly scorpions. I learned that they were deadly from a Rumanian woman whom I met and who lived nearby. She spoke some English and told me to turn on the lights at night before I went to the bathroom, or I might get bitten by one and die. I asked her why she married an Arab. She said that there was so much poverty in her country that people had to stand in a long line just to get meat or bread or any other food. Many times when you got to the front of the line the food was gone. The people were literally starving or so it sounded like that to me. So she met an Arabian and moved to Yemen where she had hoped for a better life. It must have been really bad where she lived because Yemen seemed horribly poor to me.

Mubarak usually left in the morning to go to work, or so he said, and didn't come home until late at night.

One rainy, foggy night while I was reading a book the lights went out. I wondered if the Yemenis knew what to do when there was a storm and the electricity went out. It didn't rain much in the desert except in the spring. It was March so this was the time for rain just like at home, I thought, except there wouldn't be any flowers popping up anytime soon.

I noticed that the men and children just stood outside in it as though they had never seen rain before. Nobody wore rain coats here or for that matter no coats at all.

I was thankful that I had packed a beautiful wooden candle stand that my mom had made for me. I thought of my mom as I lit the candle, put the glass over the top and crawled up in the bed and reached for my book to continue reading by the candle light. I was lucky the glass for the candle didn't break on the long trip here. Being cautious I had wrapped it in a towel before packing it in the suitcase.

I wondered when I would see my mom again. She was so far away from me now. Then I saw it in the shadows! It was crawling on the floor toward the bed. It wasn't that big, but it was a yellowish lemon color and Mubarak had told me not to let it bite me as I would die, because it was the most poisonous scorpion around. They say that most scorpions aren't that poisonous and may feel just like a bee sting, but Mubarak said that these small lemon yellow looking scorpions were deadly. He told me that just last week a man in Yemen had died from one of these crawly beasts. The local hospitals didn't have any serum to offset the poison. Later on when I did some research I discovered that these scorpions I saw were similar to a name called Leiurus quinquestriatus or the Death Stalker. This scorpion hides near human habitations in the crevices of stones and bricks and has one of the most potent venom.

I instinctively grabbed a shoe, threw it, and the tail went straight up. It was ready to attack. I grabbed another shoe and threw it. There was a thump! Fortunately, it was a direct hit. I killed it! I was so proud of myself. I happily left it there for Mubarak to see when he got home. How could he have brought me here to the land of scorpions and this lonely, unbearable, desert inhabited by deadly scorpions not to mention the wild packs of dogs growling and howling outside our house at night! I was surrounded by danger!

Mubarak told me that people couldn't keep dogs as pets because they were unclean and the angels wouldn't come into the houses with a dog inside or any other animal. I think he said that this was in the Qur'an or one of the sayings of the prophet Muhammad. "Well, somebody should do something about those dogs," I ranted. "What if the children get bit walking home from school?" "They'll probably get rabies," Mubarak mumbled.

Ironically, he brought me a healthy brown colored puppy one day, (that I called Bruce) but after two weeks he took it outside and beat it to death with a stick, and it died. I heard it yelping loudly outside one morning and went to look for him when I distinctly saw Mubarak holding a long stick in his hand and was ferociously hitting the puppy on its head. The stick must have come from my broom. I shuddered! I ran back in the house and cried for days, and this was just the beginning of what was to come. Was this really my destiny?

6. An Unexpected Tragedy

The days passed and somehow I got over Bruce and came to a realization that as long as I was married to an Arab to ever have my own puppy would be impossible.

Other things were annoying now. I was really missing hamburgers, French fries and ketchup plus getting very grouchy from being locked up in the house. I couldn't understand how any country could do without ketchup, mustard, mayonnaise, salad dressing, or anything from a bottle. I really missed my country and the food. There weren't any restaurants that allowed us to sit and eat together as a couple. Only the men were allowed to sit at the small restaurants that they had in the city of Sanaa.

It seemed to be a man's world. I didn't have anybody to speak English to but Mubarak and was finding out that he didn't understand what I was saying half the time because his English wasn't as fluent as I thought.

At this time I really needed to get out of the house and get back to working, so I decided to go to Yemen Airways and apply for a flight attendant position which is what I really wanted to do before I became a reservationist for Continental Airlines.

Unfortunately, the day I decided to apply for a job, I became very ill and found out that I was having a miscarriage. Mubarak had taken me to an Egyptian doctor whose diagnosis was that the baby was dead. He said that I was in danger of dying because my blood sugar was so low, and I needed to have surgery immediately. Mubarak said that he knew a woman who would take care of me, so he took me to her house.

I was leery about this whole situation, but I had been feeling dizzy all day and wanted to trust that my husband wouldn't want to hurt my health for our future together. We walked into an old building and continued walking up a flight of steps to her apartment. Mubarak knocked on the door, and an older lady told us to come in. She said she was expecting us. Mubarak said she was Yemeni and everything would be okay, but she couldn't promise that I would ever be able to have children again after she was done. She said that there could be complications as well from not doing this in a hospital. At least Mubarak was telling me what she said. Why had he brought me here and not taken me to a hospital? She had a long table laid out in the middle of her living room. The walls were the darkest and creepiest color of green I had ever seen. The floors were bare concrete and dingy looking. Overall, the room looked as though it hadn't been cleaned in months. As she motioned for me to get on the table I saw in her hand a huge, sharp, ancient looking bloody butcher knife among other knives lying on the table and a dirty old bucket. I was out of there! That knife looked like a sword, and there was dried blood on it. I told Mubarak that he'd better take me to the hospital, or I was going to find the American Embassy and leave him. I ran down the steps and out the door to the street to shout for a taxi. I was lucky a taxi driver suddenly pulled up by me. I heard Mubarak behind me shouting my name. The taxi driver must have heard Mubarak yelling because he got out of the car and hesitantly walked toward me. He asked what's wrong, in Arabic. I said help me. Then I fainted!

All I remember was waking up in a hospital, and a man in white was putting something that smelled really bad under my nose. It woke me up- whatever it was. Mubarak was standing over me and said the only doctor available was a Russian doctor who, of course, couldn't speak much English. I was just relieved to be taken to a hospital and thankful that Mubarak's senses finally kicked in or maybe that taxi driver helped put me in the car, and Mubarak didn't have a choice at the time. I was wheeled into a room which looked immaculately clean, so I felt much better. The doctor felt my abdomen. He knew that the baby was dead and said "dead" in English. The doctor told me that I would be okay and to count backwards from ten. I went to sleep.

When I awakened, Mubarak thought that I was dying and came running into my room. The nurse had scared him when she told him to hurry and go to my room. Somehow, day by day I got my strength back but was mentally overwhelmed by what had happened. Until this day I cry for my first baby and hope that in the next life I'll see him or her again.

Mubarak's friend came to get us from the hospital. The doctor told me to lay down in the backseat of the car on the way home. I was to stay in bed for at least a week. At this point I was wondering if I would ever want to get up again.

Mubarak said that he found a larger house, and we could move in as soon as I felt better- of course. The funny thing about Yemeni houses was that they were made of big blocks of stone which fortunately kept the house cool in the summer. Heaters weren't available, but the winters weren't that cold. They did have huge furry blankets that were made from a bear, or so Mubarak said, and were incredibly warm when it did get cold. I wish I could have one now, but I'll pass on going back to Yemen ever again.

It was becoming depressing looking out the window every morning only to see a stone wall. I wondered how the women kept their sanity being stuck in the house everyday with their only scenery being a stone wall to look at.

My guess was they had family as well as friends around whom they could visit in order to offset the loneliness.

7. The Second House and the Cat

After two weeks we finally moved into a bigger house. This house had a small garden so there was some greenery to look at which included cacti and other green strange looking pointy plants and bushes. The plants always had dust from the sand on them. Nothing ever looked pretty or clean. The sidewalks always had sand on them too. The sand would blow and stick everywhere- even on the walls of the houses.

The walls in the house, as the outside, were also made of stone, but the floors were made from marble. The marble was gray and had gold sparkles embedded in it which made the house look fancy. It felt smooth and cool when walking barefoot in the heat of the day.

One morning Mubarak brought four chickens home and let them run around in the small garden. He would chase one around, tease it, grab it by the neck and chop its head off. Yuk! Then he took it to the kitchen and threw it in a pot while taking the feathers off. I wasn't used to watching a chicken get its head chopped off so my appetite became moot. I gave up eating chicken while I lived in Yemen and not because I didn't like watching their heads being chopped off but because it tasted like rubber. The lamb and fish were much better so my diet was basically lamb, fish, rice, and salad. They didn't have salad dressing so olive oil and lemons were used for dressing. I never had any potatoes to eat probably because I never did see any potatoes at any of the little stores that Mubarak took me to. I ate them like crazy when they were served on the airplane during my working flights. How funny that a potato could become such a treat. It was almost like eating a piece of chocolate cake or cheesecake. I was becoming desperate for potatoes. I came to find out that it was a good country to live in if you wanted to lose weight because I lost about twenty pounds.

Soon after we moved into the bigger house, I learned more and more how Mubarak didn't like animals. A friend of Mubarak's gave me the cutest, fluffiest baby white kitten with huge sky blue eyes. He didn't like it, but he surprisingly let me keep it in the house. There was also a big, stray, black cat hanging around the house.

One day when Mubarak came home accompanied by a friend, he had a huge stick that he got from the yard and a big black trash bag. He told me to go to the bedroom and stay in there until he said I could come out. I was of course curious as to what he was up to so I cracked the door of the room, and saw to my amazement, that he was beating this helpless black cat with a huge stick. There was blood everywhere, and the cat was screaming and moaning. Then I saw it stop moving. I was getting sick to my stomach. Mubarak's face had an evil barbaric look that was frightening. Mubarak put the cat in a bag, and then I quietly closed the bedroom door hoping that he didn't know that I was watching. I don't know if he was showing off in front of his friend or what his motive was. It was just very morbid to kill an animal in the hallway of our house. After disposing of the cat he came back in and I peaked out the door again to see him washing the blood off the floor. I decided that I didn't want to watch anymore because the cat blood was everywhere. He never did talk to me about what he did.

The next morning I couldn't find my little white baby kitten either. I put a bowl of milk out for her, but she never came. By late afternoon I was getting worried about her. Mubarak said that it probably ran away, but I thought that he probably had killed it as well. Thoughts kept coming to my mind that if he did this to animals, would he do this to people too!

8. Being a Flight Attendant

One day when Mubarak came home he said that Yemen Airways was hiring flight attendants and that he would take me to the office if I wanted to apply. I said okay, and the next day I had an interview with a Yemeni woman who hired me to go through flight attendant training.

I met a lot of girls from different countries when I was taking my training. Two best friends that I made were from Delhi and Bombay, India. When I first met them they asked me to sit by them. Tanya, the younger, about my age was very cute with black eyes and short black hair. Tanya was very inquisitive about America. She acted as though she wanted to get on a plane right now and live there if she could. Geraldine was very calm and easy to talk to. She also had dark brown eyes and long black hair. She too was very cute, polite, and friendly. On our days off they would come to my house and stay with me. We would talk all night, and I felt like they were becoming like sisters to me. To this day I miss them very much, and wish I could see them again.

Surprisingly, their English was excellent! It was great to meet people who spoke English after such a long time. They were Christians unlike most of the others who were Hindu or believed in nature. They came to work as long as they could to send money home to their families and eventually go back to India to get married.

I distinctly remember that the Indians didn't care much for the Egyptian flight attendants. They told me not to hang around with them, but I did anyway. I met six of them, and they invited me to their apartment. They were also very friendly. Two of them spoke English extremely well. Their names were Jeehan and Ashgan, Nejawah, and Sahar. Jeehan was the most outgoing. She had curly long brown hair and honey brown eyes. She was more heavyset and shorter than the other girls, but very pretty. Jeehan's features truly made her look like an Egyptian. Ashgan had light brown hair and was slightly taller than her sister. She was about five foot six. They both had beautiful olive colored skin. They looked like they had been sunbathing at the beach for a couple of months. Ashgan liked to go out and party every night and soon got herself in trouble for doing so, because Yemen is not a place where women should be out at night. Nejwah and Sahar were very nice and more talkative once I got to know them better. They both had black hair and were much lighter in complexion. I loved to watch them do their eyes with black eyeliner. Charcoal was sometimes used instead of eyeliner as another method but was used more so in the past even in the days when King Tut was around. They taught me how to do my eyes as the Egyptians do which really makes ones eyes look mysteriously bigger. Of course that was the whole point of the black eyeliner.

Jeehan and Ashgan said they studied English in London when they were younger. They cooked for me and liked to go out shopping and socialize with anybody and everybody. I loved the molokheiya that they made. It is spinach cooked with chicken or lamb. They told me that molokheiya was eaten by the Pharoahs. I did some research and discovered that it really was eaten by the Egyptian Pharoahs. It is called Egyptian spinach.

I was surprised that they knew the song "Walk like an Egyptian." They also were the ones who taught me how to belly dance, and were they ever good at it! They tied colorful scarves around their waists as well as me and showed me how to move my body to the Arabian music. It was fun and good exercise too! They had the best sense of humor, and until this day I've never met anybody who I had as much fun with as these girls-except for some of my friends who went to high school with me. They tried to teach me how to speak Arabic, but the Egyptian dialect was really hard to understand. I was just getting used to how the

Yemeni's spoke, and Mubarak was teaching me the language, but the different dialect was getting me confused again.

Mubarak decided that it was time for us to get married in the Islamic religion. I got the impression this was because of his mom as she had spoken to Mubarak and said that we should be married in their religion "so it would be right." The following week an Islamic priest came to the house to marry us. The priest had long white hair and a long white beard. He could have passed for the prophet Noah if I would have seen his ark outside the window.

My Egyptian and Indian friends all came and so did his Yemeni friends. It was a small wedding, and Mubarak and I were the only ones in the room with the priest when he married us. Following the ceremony we had a reception at our house while all of my friends brought food and cake. One of my Egyptian friends made necklaces of real flowers. She gave one to everybody. She even put them on the men. Mubarak's friends killed a lamb, and we had lamb and rice for the main course. Actually, Mubarak killed the lamb with his friends. They performed this task in our bathroom. That was a bloody sight to see, and yes, in our bathroom!

For a wedding gift, Mubarak gave me a set of gold jewelry and beautiful sequined laced dresses of different colors that were sent from his family in Riyadh, Saudi Arabia. It was a nice wedding, and Mubarak seemed to be a lot happier since we were finally married in the Islamic religion.

After we got married it was back to flight attendant training which was going well, and I was almost finished and getting ready to get my license from the civil aviation. First, I had to be tested. I didn't know that I had to climb out of a window of a 747 and jump off the wing that was unbelievably high up, but I did it without breaking a leg or any other bone for that matter. We also had to slide down an emergency shoot from the back of the plane. If you didn't keep your feet pointed up as you exited the plane, there would be a major flip with your body. That is exactly what happened to a few of the girls, and they had to do it over until they got it right. We also had to pass a swimming test that was easy for me since my mom made me take swimming lessons from the time I was five years old. We took our swimming test at the Queen of Sheba Hotel which I presumed was named after the one and only

Queen of Sheba. Thank goodness my teacher was from Canada so her English was excellent which made the class a lot more interesting. My teacher stood out in a crowd in Yemen with her white blond hair and blue eyes. It didn't seem to bother her though and ignored the men that acted childish when they saw her. I must say that I learned a lot about people and their cultures by meeting so many people of different nationalities.

I was thrilled when I finally received my flight attendant license. My first flight was on a 737. I flew to a small town, if I remember correctly, called Hodeida? It was a very dry, mountainous desert region. We had a layover and had to spend the night there. I wondered if it was because of the rain because we were supposed to be back in Riyadh by that night. We drove to a hotel which was on top of a mountain. We parked our bus at the bottom and had to walk a million steps to get to the top. I looked around and saw nothing. The whole area looked deserted only desert could be seen for miles. As I looked up at the hotel it was kind of creepy. It reminded me of Dracula's castle high up on a mountain like you see in a horror movie.

Of course with my bad luck something was bound to happen tonight. My intuition was telling me so. And I was right because as soon as I got settled in my room there was a knock on the door. I opened the door and the co-pilot let himself in. I could tell by his breath that he had been drinking. He asked if I wanted something to eat. He said they made really good fish at this hotel. I told him that I was planning to order for the room and eat alone and then get some rest before our flight tomorrow. He insisted on staying. He picked up the phone and ordered some dinner. He said that we could eat and then he would leave. As we ate he drank a whole bottle of scotch. He told me to drink. He said that all Americans drink. I said, "No not all of them." I told him that I didn't want to drink since we had to get up early for a long flight. He said that he would have a couple of drinks and leave. I told him that sounded like a bunch of bologna to me. He didn't understand what that meant and asked me what bologna was. Of course I thought everybody knew what bologna was, but evidently they didn't.

He said that all Americans like to have fun and party. I said, "This American needs sleep to work on a plane tomorrow. Working on a plane flying at forty thousand feet with a hangover is not something that I would ever want to try. It was hard enough at times to keep my balance in a healthy condition." I'm sure he would find out what it would be like tomorrow.

I was getting angry by now and asked him where he got his information that all Americans do is party. I told him it was time to leave, but he wouldn't. I started getting angry as he became more drunk and pushy. He said that all American women are really prostitutes. I told him that is a terrible thing to say about all American women. I said, "Who has taught you such a thing?" He said everybody in the Middle East believes that. I told him that he knew very well that I was married and that I would call security if he didn't leave. I tried to push him out the door, but he pushed the door back open. I kicked him and pushed him out again. He threw the door back open. He knocked me over and fell on top of me. Then I smacked him in the face and pushed him away. He didn't move. I was hoping that he had passed out. I decided to call the pilot since he had told me to call him if I needed any help with anything. The pilot said that he would be over to my room right away. I quickly drug the co-pilot out into the hall. The pilot came and asked what happened. I told him that this man wouldn't leave me alone and then he passed out. He said that he would take care of it and not to open my door for him anymore. I said thanks for the tip, but how was I supposed to know that this man was going to attack me. Are all the Arabs over here like this? The pilot nodded his head. Yes! "All of them except me." He said that he's married to an American and is very happy. I was shocked because I didn't know that he was married to an American. Who would have guessed? I presumed that I shouldn't talk to any men at all or they would continuously bother me. What a great way to start my first day as a flight attendant. I decided that this man wasn't going to mess up my career.

I woke up early in the morning. I was hoping that what's his name wasn't going to fly the plane. I put my uniform on and was hoping to sneak out of the hotel without seeing him. I saw the captain and walked down to our bus with him. He said that he hadn't seen the co-pilot yet. I didn't answer. We had to wait for the co-pilot after we were settled on the bus. The pilot seemed a bit upset after fifteen minutes had passed and no co-pilot. Finally he came and didn't look very good to say the least. I was glad that he didn't sit by me.

As we boarded the plane and took off for Riyadh, I took the captain and co-pilot some coffee and breakfast. The pilot was smoking a pipe and told me to sit down. He told me to listen to what he was going to say because he wanted to teach me about the flight instruments and what to do if there was an emergency. He showed me the radar and told me that if we went through the dark cloud on the left that it would tear the plane apart. I said, "Well don't go that way!"

The co-pilot never said a word. The pilot said that he wasn't going to let the co-pilot fly the plane after what happened the previous night. He wasn't in a good condition to fly. I just nodded. The pilot told me to keep bringing the co-pilot coffee and tea and maybe a bucket. I would have liked to put a bucket on his head, but I said okay and shut the cockpit door. After we landed and the passengers left the co-pilot asked if I wanted to take a two-week flight to Germany with him. I said, "Not with you." He said that he could arrange it so that we would have time to go sight-seeing. I repeated myself and said, "Not with you." I said, "I'll wait until the office arranges it for me, but not with you on the flight." "I told you that I'm married." "Can't you get it through your head?" He continued to follow me. When I got to the office I called Mubarak to come and pick me up at the airport. He did, and the co-pilot immediately left me alone. I never did fly with him again and was thankful that maybe the pilot made sure that we weren't ever on the same plane again.

The next few domestic flights that I had were interesting as well. There always seemed to be green leaves and bushes all over the plane. I learned that these were Khat leaves from a tree that are rather bitter-tasting. The people chew the leaves for the stimulants in them, and it is a very popular part of social life for the Yemeni people.

The floor of the plane looked like a jungle, and I couldn't believe this was allowed. I had to get used to tripping over prickly branches and huge green leaves while I walked through the aisles. Later on, I found out that these leaves that they put in their mouths and chewed were a kind of drug that was supposed to be relaxing or make them high.

On one trip going home the plane started swaying and going down causing me to jut forward and fall on the floor. I heard the pilot say "Please fasten your seatbelts." "This includes all flight attendants." Now he tells us after we all fall. The plane took a nose dive causing the oxygen masks to descend. Luckily, I pulled myself up from the floor and grabbed an empty passenger seat in time and buckled myself in. But my partner wasn't so lucky. She went flying forward again and sprained one of her legs. The plane leveled out fairly quickly, and the passengers remained relatively calm. There must have been some strong calming agent in that khat to keep them so quiet. That was one of the scariest flights that I had experienced. Later I discovered that the pilot and co-pilot were chewing khat while they were flying. How could this be legal while flying a plane? I guess they felt they could get away with it, and I just hoped that we wouldn't crash and all be killed. The other flight attendants were angry to say the least. They knew that the pilots were chewing khat while flying the plane. When I finally had my chance to give the pilots their food and drinks, sure enough there were leaves and branches in the cockpit as well. The proof was "in the pudding," as we say back home.

The next few flights were to Jeddah and Mecca which was where the Arabs were going to make their Hajj. I wondered what in the world that was. Everybody was wearing white rags, and they smelled like they hadn't had a shower in weeks.

The women were wrapped in white rags as well that looked like sheets (Mubarak told me that they were sheets.) which was a definite change from the black capes normally worn. I learned that Muslims were required to make Hajj once in their lifetime, and they went to the Kaba in Mecca to fulfill this commandment. All Muslims would walk in circles around the Kaba from morning until night praying asking for forgiveness of their sins. This was called their Pilgrimage. As a result of this, the plane was packed traveling back and forth from Riyadh to Jeddah, and I had to do double shifts. After two days without sleep I was thankful for our relief when the next group of flight attendants came on duty.

My next flight was to Cyprus and Larnica in Greece. This was a longer flight on board a 747 and took about seven hours. I liked this flight because I knew for one thing there would be food served, and the flight attendants were allowed to have lunch, too. There were potatoes, rice, lamb, beef, chicken, fish, and every kind of fruit that I could think of. I really missed eating potatoes, so it was a treat for me. The chicken didn't taste like plastic. It was full of flavor on this flight. Fortunately, there wasn't any khat (the green leaves) to walk over, but there was a criminal who was being transported on the plane. I, of course, was the one who had to take him water and food for the entire flight. I didn't see his handcuffs at first, and he told me to sit down beside him. I told him that I was working and asked what he wanted. When he insisted that I sit down I noticed the handcuffs. Just then the policeman came up front carrying his gun in front of him and told me to bring them some water. I asked the girls why they didn't tell me that I had to tend to the criminal. They just laughed and said, "Because you are an American, you are not afraid of anything." I said, "Yeah, right." They said that they were too afraid of being hurt or something worse could happen. I wondered, "Did we as Americans really portray what everyone said? Did all the Arabs think that we were brave partying people? Is that what we were?" That's all I ever heard- we were courageous and liked to party. Of course they thought most of us were atheist, too. I was going to get to the bottom of this, especially about the part that most Americans are atheist. I think that our country is blessed being able to choose whatever we want to believe in and not get our heads chopped off because of our beliefs. We make our own choices in this life and will have to suffer the consequences for them or not. I had only met one true atheist in my life, and she was a very nice trustworthy person.

Some of the girls told me that they didn't like to fly on the little planes because they said it made them sick to their stomachs and they would start vomiting. I was called many times to take a flight attendant's place on my days off to replace someone that couldn't continue their flight. How could a person be a flight attendant if he or she kept getting sick? That seemed really dumb to me, but I guess it couldn't be helped.

Greece was amazingly beautiful! As we were landing the sun was just rising over the mountains. Our hotel was on top of a mountain but it was beautiful unlike Yemen. It was nice to see some greenery.

I was rooming with Ashgan, my Egyptian girlfriend, and she was ready to go out and explore the city. The fresh air was exhilarating and the chill in the air kept me going from lack of sleep. It was a very hilly place to walk, and the streets were lined with old looking buildings. It was as if we were walking straight down a mountain which I guess we were. We both tripped a couple of times since we were wearing high heels. Of course, we shopped for hours and then went sight- seeing. There were a lot of shops to go in and out of, and the food was excellent. They had Schwarma's which were pita wraps loaded with mayonnaise, salad and stuffed with lamb or chicken rolled up inside. They even had French fries which of course we both loved. After being awake for twenty-four hours and walking around all day, we were exhausted, and finally went back to the hotel to get some sleep.

Eventually, I was assigned to a Cairo, Egypt flight, but we had a short layover, and the pilots just gave us enough time to go to the hotel to eat before we had to leave. However, I did see the Pyramids from the plane. They were an amazing sight from the sky as they jutted up from the earth surrounded by only desert. They seemed smaller than I had imagined, but I was looking down from ten to fifteen thousand feet. I never did get a chance to go inside the Pyramids which I sometimes regret as I don't know if I'll ever get back there again. At the time I thought that since I lived so close that I would eventually be able to go sight-seeing in Egypt, but it's not that easy when you're continuously working and your life keeps changing.

The trips that I enjoyed the most were the ones to Abu Dhabi and Dubai in the United Arab Emirates. It was like paradise there with the white beaches and the serene waterfalls surrounding the pools. There was beautiful green grass that surrounded the hotels. The women also had more freedom, or so I found out after watching a belly dancer in the lounge of the hotel one night. I thought that might be more fun than being a flight attendant: Wishful thinking. She was really entertaining to watch and was a really good dancer.

When you're a flight attendant staying in one place for long doesn't happen. When we traveled to Dubai, I remember one of the flight attendants (whose name was Nadia) telling me that if the plane crashes over Dubai, the life rafts wouldn't save us because we would be eaten alive by the sharks. Then I looked down and sure enough the ocean was just festering with sharks. There must have been hundreds near the shore. The water was the lightest, greenish- blue color that I had ever seen, so the sharks were quite visible. She said the shark repellent wouldn't help much because there were too many. Just when she said that, we hit an air pocket and the plane dropped suddenly. I said, "So where is that shark repellent because it might buy me a little time to swim to shore?" Nadia showed me where it was stored and just laughed. Nadia was from Egypt. I liked her a lot. I decided this was the name that I was going to give to my little girl when she was born. I learned a lot from Nadia about working on the plane, and she was also a good friend. She was one of the head flight attendants and soon moved me up to first class where I went to the cockpit on the 747s to serve the pilots. The pilots soon let me sit up front with them to watch the take-offs and landings and showed me the different control panels and how to fly the plane.

When I flew to Khartoum and Addis Ababa the people had very dark complexions and covered their heads in turbans. The land looked so dreadfully dry and barren that gave the appearance of being a very poor country. The people, however, were very polite and said thank you when we served them, unlike the Yemenis whom I served on other flights. I liked the Yemenis, and it wasn't their fault they weren't as lucky to be educated like I was where education is imperative as well as mandatory in the United States.

When I was nineteen years old, I had no idea there were so many diverse people and countries to see. How fortunate I was to be able to be a flight attendant in the Middle East, but of all places for this to happen—who would have thought? At times I wondered why Mubarak let me travel and spend the night away from him. Oddly, he never asked me about my trips. For some reason he seemed preoccupied in Yemen— for the time being anyhow. At times he would be very angry about everything, and I knew that he didn't have a job and was depending on me to give him money which he didn't like, but there wasn't any choice at the time. I knew he was fed up living in Yemen.

One day while we were having a disagreement, he took his whole arm, swung it, and hit me in the face, and blood started gushing out of my nose. My eye became bruised as well. I never knew how painful it was to be boxed in the nose. The blood didn't stop for awhile. I sat on the couch and held my nose with a rag knowing that I didn't deserve to be hit. Shortly after that incident he finally got me a visa to get into

Riyadh, Saudi Arabia. Unfortunately, I had to give up being a flight attendant and move on. His parents were evidently begging him to come back to live there. They were anxious to meet me, the American wife.

9. His Family

I was nineteen years old now. As soon as we arrived in Riyadh, we went directly to Mubarak's parent's house. Downtown Riyadh was a very big city, but his family's house was in a small rural area next to the desert located approximately thirty minutes from the city. Their house was near the end of an eerie, old street. Many of the houses looked decrepit and uninhabited, including his family home. I guessed that this must have been the slums of Riyadh. I thought his family was doing so much better the way Mubarak had talked. I was wondering what happened. As we drove through the slums Mubarak told me that his father's factory had gone bankrupt and was closed down.

It was a late December afternoon when we reached their house. His mother, whose name is Barka, opened the door abruptly. I didn't see her at first, but I heard her voice. She was standing behind the door. It just dawned on me that women weren't allowed to show themselves without wearing their black capes and veils so that's why she was behind the door. My husband walked in and disappeared with his mother. I nervously stood alone inside the house by the door for a short while. Soon his mother came back and motioned for me to go into a small, austere room to the right. Then she hugged me and started speaking Arabic. I only stood there not knowing what to do or say. I only knew a few Arabic words, and at that time I was becoming very uncomfortable. As my tension began to grow, suddenly my mother-in-law started moving her hands in all directions as she spoke. I presumed she wanted me to sit down, so I sat. Then she smiled and sat down too. I smiled back and discreetly looked at her. They didn't have any furniture in the room, except I immediately noticed the cushions along the wall and the carpet as she motioned me to sit on the floor. There was also a small cabinet with a television in it. The walls looked like they were made of cement and painted green. It was sort of like being in a cave. It reminded me of when I used to go in the haunted houses when I was younger. I was waiting for somebody to jump out with a mask on and scare me. It was definitely creepy.

Barka was about five foot four with long black hair that reached her waist. It was pulled back in a pony tail. She had beautiful olive skin, and her eyes looked black. She had very distinct facial features. The dress that she was wearing covered her feet almost completely. She gave me a stern look, grinned, and started speaking Arabic. I was beginning to get a little upset not being able to understand her at all. Finally, Mubarak walked in and began interpreting what his mother said. I started feeling more at ease; however, I realized that she was determined to communicate with me whether her son was around or not. His mother emphasized that I needed to learn more Arabic right away. She was definitely not reticent about her opinions. My husband left the room again with his mother following a few steps behind.

After a few minutes, two young girls walked in bringing a tray with tea and another with cakes and snacks. They put the trays in the middle of the room on the floor and came over to shake my hand. They started speaking Arabic. I said I didn't understand, and they both smiled. They tried to speak to me again, and I said, "I don't understand." Then they put their hands to their mouths like they were eating and drinking. They wanted me to move closer to them and eat. They were very beautiful young teenagers with long black hair and the biggest dark brown eyes I had ever seen. They appeared to be close in age, around fifteen and sixteen. They were a bit taller than their mother. Suddenly, the one who looked the youngest made a square figure with her hands while she was speaking. I had no idea what she was trying to tell me. Then she got up, went to the television, and acted like she was turning it on. She was asking if I wanted to watch the television. They looked at me, whispered quietly and then laughed. I felt so out of place not being able to communicate, but they both gave me a huge smile, and I felt better. Their mother came back and sat down for some tea. She moved her hands to her mouth as though she was eating. I knew she wanted me to eat the cake. After I ate a piece, she put another one in my hand. Next, she pointed to the tea cup and put her hand to her mouth like she was drinking. She wanted me to drink some tea, of course. I politely took a cup of tea and smiled. Then my mother-in-law said, "Momma America?" I nodded my head up and down euphorically to finally understand something and reply that yes, my mom was in America and she, my mom, was probably thinking what a crazy daughter she had to want to go to Saudi Arabia. I tried to ask the girls what their names were. The one girl, Jameliah, was very quick and responded immediately, "My name is Jameliah and this is Fatima." Being facetious, my mother-in-law pointed to herself and said, "Momma," Everybody started laughing. I was finally feeling more comfortable, and their sense of humor helped immensely. Mubarak's mother was definitely not shy, so I was beginning to wonder how things were going to work out with me not being a Muslim and not being able to speak any Arabic. Mubarak soon returned and asked how I was doing? I said, "Much better." He sat down on the soft, beautiful Arabian rug and began to translate what his mother and sisters were saying.

As the years went by, I found many ingenious ways to communicate until I could speak Arabic fluently. Although after fourteen years, when I was able to speak fluently, there were times when I still looked at them with a blank face. We would laugh, and they would show me a picture, an object, or act out what they wanted to tell me until I understood.

Mubarak's family killed a lamb the next day in honor of their son coming back home safely with a new bride. They made lamb with rice, and the entire family sat down together. I was relieved that I didn't have to cover my hair in their home because his brothers and father were allowed to see me. I learned that lamb with rice was their traditional meal that would always be served at weddings and special occasions. This dish was called kupsa in Arabic. They served it with a salad of chopped tomatoes, onions, lettuce, cucumbers, carrots, and parsley that was all chopped very small together in a huge bowl. The dressing was lemons that were squeezed on the top with olive oil and salt and pepper. They also put hot peppers out for whoever was daring enough to eat them. Mubarak usually ate the peppers and encouraged me to start eating some, too. The meals were eaten on the floor. The women would put a thin layer of plastic across the floor as far as would be needed to serve as a tablecloth. After the meal, tea and cake would be eaten on the floor as well, or they might sit on cushions that were put around the walls of the living room. The house to me was very old and creepy, and at night I told Mubarak that I bet if we stay up late enough we might see a ghost passing by. He said that could be a possibility since the graveyard was close by, and some people that live near graveyards hear screams in the night coming from the graves. The middle of the house was open without a roof so when it rained it rained inside the house and into the living room where we would eat our meals. That sounds weird, but that's the way it was. Can you imagine it raining in your living room? They had a plastic green grass carpet covering on the floor, so when it rained they rolled it up and put it away. Everybody would sit in the other smaller closed rooms or bedrooms when it rained. Mubarak and I would run through the living room in the rain to go upstairs to our bedroom. We were soaked by the time we got upstairs to our room. I thought to myself, "This is really strange!" I told him that we need to get an umbrella to take with us when walk down to the kitchen to get something to drink or eat.

We did have a nice big bedroom, but the bathroom was another thing altogether. There was just a hole in the floor for the toilet so you can imagine how that was. Furthermore, they didn't have or use toilet paper. Toilet paper was something that the Americans used, and it didn't clean a person good enough. Mubarak said it's better to wash which the Americans don't know how to do. The Muslims didn't do as the caphers (atheists) did. They had a hose or a bidet (that's the name in Arabic) to wash with. Later on I found out that the other houses in the city had regular American toilets with French toilets next to them that had a spray in it. The houses that I had seen or lived in had the toilets with a hole in the ground. They were surrounded by different colors of marble which helped as it didn't look like just a plain hole in the floor. I think that should explain the toilets over there fairly well. They did have sinks which were made of marble or porcelain as well. They didn't have hot water upstairs, so we usually would take cold or lukewarm showers. The water would get warmer during the day when it was hot outside, so I would wait until the afternoon to shower.

Mubarak's mom was very friendly toward me, but I often wondered what she thought of me or said when I wasn't around. My dad told me "That people can be very nice when they talk to you, but when you turn your back that's when they start talking bad about you." My dad drove me nuts when he talked like that. It was so deep, and I'd rather not think that people thought bad things about me. I've always liked everybody that I have ever met except when they show me otherwise. I liked Barka and was hoping that she felt the same!

She was an excellent cook, and there was always plenty of food to eat. She knew how to cook Hindi, Saudi, Lebanese, Palestinian, Yemeni, American, and other Arabic food as well. She also taught me how to cook for fifty people or more. She could have had her own television food network as good as she was at cooking and entertaining.

One day for lunch she made a roast that included gravy with potatoes, onions, and carrots just for me. The meat was lamb, but the way she made it was amazingly close to tasting just like roast beef. I was impressed! She said that I seemed sad at times and thought that I might be missing home, so she made an American dish for me. She was reading my mind because I was missing home and our traditional food. I told her thank you (shookron) in Arabic and gave her a hug.

Mubarak's dad was usually quiet when I was around and just nodded and smiled at me. This continued for most of the fourteen years that I was around. Maybe he didn't really know how to communicate with me. I guess I'll never know. His name was Salem (if I didn't mention it yet) and Mubarak wanted a baby named Salem that we never had. I was glad that Salem was always very hospitable and civilized with me, but then again who knows what he said behind my back. He did seem to love his grandchildren that I had given him even though they were part American. I never heard him complain even once. He was proud and called them beautiful, white Amerikia babies. He had more curly hair then Mubarak that was now turning gray. He of course had a moustache like all the other Arabian men who I had seen. I wondered what they all would look like without one. He was about the height of Mubarak, and there was some resemblance of his son. Although I thought Mubarak looked and acted more like his mother. I noticed that he smoked a lot, but most Arabian men that I had met so far smoked quite a bit. He didn't seem to be much of a gossiper. He said things as he thought and that was that. If the women spoke and he didn't like what they said he would leave the room. He told Mubarak that I needed to learn more Arabic and become a Muslim. Mubarak told him that I would learn about Islam and speak Arabic. I just needed some time. Mubarak didn't seem to be in a hurry to teach me Arabic which was frustrating in the beginning.

Mubarak and I would sit up late at night and watch television. Mubarak loved to watch the old comedies like Abbot and Costello. I had no idea how he knew who they were until I discovered that old movies were all that they showed in Arabia when they first had television so Mubarak said.

His temper seemed to subside since we were living with his parents. I thought that incident of him hitting me in Yemen was maybe just a cry for help.

One night we were lying in bed, and ten or more tiny, gray mice crawled up on top of our blanket. I counted them quickly of course. I instinctively jumped up and screamed. What was with the mice around here? After that I didn't want to fall asleep for fear they would surround me, but of course that didn't happen. Mubarak promised that they wouldn't hurt me. He said, "They are babies and just cold." "All animals are from Allah and to not be afraid." That was weird, but they never bit me. I had to learn to sleep with baby mice on top of my blanket every night from then on. What a strange life I had. Who would have believed me if I told them?

I wanted to go out alone and go shopping one day, but I soon learned that women were not permitted to drive in Riyadh. While I was living in Riyadh there were approximately one hundred princesses who conspired to drive through the city. They tricked their chauffeurs to get out of the car and took off with it. When the princesses drove down the main highway of Riyadh, the police arrested all of them and took them to jail. There were many rumors that the princesses were beaten while they were in jail. One prince ordered his wife to be executed. Sadly, she was beheaded. During the years that I lived there, no other attempt to drive by women had ever been made since this calamity. There were many times that I wanted to drive. I remember putting on Mubarak's white robe and his traditional head scarf, but I started thinking that all the men in Riyadh had moustaches. I decided that I couldn't make a good enough disguise and was worried that my accent in Arabic wasn't quite good enough yet. Mubarak told me that the court would have me executed if I was caught driving. They wouldn't care if I was an American or not. I decided against driving and became used to having my own driver.

10. Back to the States

After staying with Mubarak's family for a couple of months, we decided to go back to the United States again. Our plans were to go to Washington D.C. to stay with my sisters. It was December and I was twenty years old now. I left first which was nice because I had a layover in Madrid, Spain for three days.

I was so naïve how I thought that all nationalities would naturally speak great English wherever I went. Of course I found out that nobody I met spoke English, or if they did it was only a few words. Even the people at the hotel where I was staying just couldn't seem to understand what in the world I was saying, but I somehow got through with visuals and sign language just like I had to do in Arabia. I was just desperate in my heart and mind to get back home to speak to people who would be able to converse with me. How I so took that for granted. I was walking around mumbling to myself how friendly Americans were and most of these other people from different countries can't even say hi or smile. Americans always say hi. Was it so hard to smile and greet somebody? I decided that I could stick my nose up in the air too and not say hi, but I thought that's not from where I came from to be unfriendly. I kept smiling and tried to communicate with my hands or broken English or whatever I could. It seemed to get me where I needed to go or what I wanted.

I anxiously went to my hotel room and was hoping to find toilet paper and a wash cloth, but oh no there wasn't either one there. I took a huge towel to use as a wash cloth in the shower with me to wash and had to, of course, use the bidet or French toilet as usual. We as Americans I learned seem to have ways to get by to survive when necessary.

How I missed America and everything that it had to offer, especially toilet paper, clean water, ketchup, mustard, mayonnaise, hamburgers, hotdogs and anything and everything. It was definitely the land of plenty, or was I just spoiled?

It was getting late and I was hungry. I decided to go to the hotel restaurant and get something to eat. The tables were covered with white tablecloths and romantic, white candles were lit. I was wishing that I wasn't alone. Of course the waiter didn't know English. I couldn't read the menu in a foreign language except when I saw spaghetti. Spaghetti sounded good I told the waiter. Thankfully, he understood that. He brought me a big flask of red wine, bread, and a huge salad which I didn't order, but I decided that I might as well indulge because when will I ever be back in Spain again? However, I did try to tell him that I didn't order anything but spaghetti. My interpretation of what he said was that the wine and bread come with the meal, but "I didn't order the salad either." He didn't reply but smiled. The wine was excellent. Next, the waiter brought spaghetti and the biggest meatballs I had ever seen. It was too much food! I was hoping that it wasn't going to be a hundred dollar meal for all of it. Everybody I seemed to meet takes for granted that all Americans are rich. Well the meal wasn't cheap, but fairly reasonable compared to the dollar, thank goodness. I realized there were so many things said about us Americans that weren't completely true or not true at all. I imagine we also have our own ideas about foreigners though. Although I do feel that it is quite ridiculous that the Arabs I had met think that most or all Americans are atheist and or prostitutes. We as Americans are a mixture of many cultures of people and have many good qualities no matter whom or what we are. I didn't think we should be labeled as such.

Once, I remember sitting around with Mubarak's sisters and they were watching satellite television. The channel was showing college students on the beach in Florida during Spring Break and the girls wearing short skirts and bikinis. Jamelia (Mubarak's sister) laughed and said that they must have run out of material to finish making their clothes. His sisters said that they looked like prostitutes not wearing hardly anything, and they needed to cover their bodies. I had to admit that some bikinis did look a bit skimpy. When I was a teenager I wore bikinis too, but they were jumping to conclusions about the prostitute thing. I remember wearing a bikini to the beach when I went on a trip with my family to Florida and didn't think anything about it, nor did my dad or anybody else for that matter. Then why was I feeling so guilty and ashamed about wearing a bikini and apologizing for the girls on television? I decided that maybe I was becoming brainwashed from their views of American life.

I was always so proud of being an American, but I was coming to a realization that I was just a foreigner in Spain or any other country. I now had to abide by the laws of these countries. I decided that it was time to go to my hotel room and get some sleep and try to stop analyzing everybody and everything.

By the next afternoon I was longing to take a walk. It was late in the day since I was still living the Arabian life. Most people slept late in Arabia and stayed up late. Mubarak, and his family did anyway because that was what they were accustomed to. I strolled down an old, cobbled street. There were many shops, cafés, and a big shopping mall that I saw as I went sight-seeing. There was what looked like a bakery, but the people were standing outside selling food. I looked at what they were selling, and it looked just like samboosa (fried phyllo dough with meat inside). It seemed strange that the people in Spain would make similar food as the Arabs, but they were fairly close to each other after all these centuries of traveling. I didn't feel like eating Arabic food at the time, so I took a plain boring chicken sandwich on a bun and kept walking. I went to the mall which was very modernized. I walked around for a couple of hours as it was getting dark. I was getting hungry, but nothing looked good as I walked down another old cobbled street. I looked down at the street and saw that the brick was cracked in many places, but there was beauty in this brick maybe no one could see, but I could. It showed the age of this country and its history. I decided to wander around which to this day I wonder what I was thinking. I was only twenty, a foreigner, walking alone on a back alley at about eleven o'clock at night. The next thing I knew I was lost-so many alleys and they all looked the same. If I could just find those little shops with the bakery, I would be okay. I gasped with surprise when I saw a gang of rough looking guys wearing black leather jackets and black leather pants coming towards me, swinging big silver chains. Now what? Yell help! Who would hear me? They took a glance at me and then walked right past me and didn't say anything, but I was getting worried because the further I walked the rougher the guys were looking. Then I saw some older people who looked like tourists—possibly. I followed them, and luckily they went right to that little bakery and got something to eat. I was lucky that time and decided not to wander off on anymore back alleys alone. My curiousness kept getting me in trouble or close to it. I decided to get another sandwich and call it a night. Tomorrow I was going to Washington D.C., and I was more than ready to go back home to the so called evil toilet paper, prostitutes, and atheists or whatever all the foreigners or Arabs that I met thought of us—which of course isn't true of everybody, and I don't believe that everybody thought of us that way. The Americans were my people, and I loved every human being that spoke English or whatever language or nationality spoken in America. At least we were a free country, and isn't that what God said anyway? We have a choice to choose whatever way it may be good or evil and thus our consequences would be given.

I arrived in Washington late one night, and of course my sisters were late arriving to pick me up. I presumed they were sitting at a bar, knowing those two. I was right. As they walked toward me I could tell they were laughing and joking and falling over each other. My sisters knew how to have a good time at one happy point and time in our lives. It made me happy though to see them laughing and getting along so well not like our lives today.

They asked how long I had sat waiting for them. I said, "About an hour." "Where in the world have you two been?" They laughed again and said they were sorry that they were a little late. They both replied, "We got off work late, and you know we went to the bar because it looked like your flight was going to be late." I said, "I figured that's where you were." "Welcome back to America," they said. Looking at my two sisters, whom I love dearly, I realized that some nationalities could possibly get the wrong idea about us as crazy as some of us acted at times. This was my country though, hardworking, carefree, and happy, fun- loving people for the most part.

My sisters (Randa and Lisa) were both working for MCI (American Telecommunications Company) at the time. My one sister, Lisa was dating a Secret Service agent. That sounded exciting! My other sister was going through a divorce and evidently almost died by being thrown through a window and still had huge scar marks all over her body. "Lucky girl to be alive," My dad said about my oldest sister when I saw him again. He always said that, and I bet he said that to himself after I got back from Arabia.

As I look back my sisters were very hospitable to let Mubarak and me come and live with them. We would have our own room, and they would sleep in another room. I think we all were going through trying times. Strange how life is like my mom says, "When it rains, it pours." It sure seemed to pour on me a lot.

One night my sister Randa refused to open her bedroom door. Lisa and I got this hunch to try to open her door with a bobby pin and anything else we could. She yelled at us to leave her alone. Lisa was worried about her and kept trying to open the door with that darn pin. Finally, we managed to open the door, and we also got a tongue lashing from our older sister who threw a book at us and said to get out. She said that she was okay and just wanted to read a book in peace. (She is a voracious reader.) So we left her alone.

About a week after Mubarak arrived we stayed up at night thinking that this was going to be a huge mistake; I felt it coming. Mubarak wanted to work in a bank or a business somewhere and couldn't find anything but a job as a waiter in a restaurant downtown. He said that he didn't want to be a waiter for the rest of his life, ironically, we moved back to Houston to rent an apartment with his uncle Omar who was living there at the time. After about a month his uncle got him into some sort of trouble. I found out about it when two CIA agents came to our apartment one morning.

A friend had stopped by and told Mubarak that he needed to get out of the apartment right away. Mubarak ran to the living room and I saw him go out the door. I shut the door to the bedroom wondering what was going on. I heard some men in the living room when suddenly the bedroom door was kicked open by one of the agents.

He grabbed me and put a big gun to the side of my head while telling me to walk slowly into our living room. I was so hoping that the gun wouldn't go off as hard as he was pushing it into my head. Did he really have to push it that hard? I was thinking to myself. Why me, why always me? The other agent said, "Leave her alone!" when they found Mubarak. The agent moved the gun away from my head and pointed it at Mubarak. They put handcuffs on him and took him away to jail. In the meantime the only other thing that I knew to do was to go back home, even though Mubarak's uncle Omar tried to persuade me to go with him to Mexico to live. Fortunately, the gun put to my head must have knocked some common sense into me because I chose to go home to clear my head from all of these horrible things that kept happening to me. I called my mom and told her what happened, and she sent me a ticket to fly home. I don't know what I would have done without my mom who always picked me up after falling. After having children of my own now, I know why she helped me. No matter what happens, a mother's love is always there.

After being home for a couple of months I knew a decision would have to be made about my life with Mubarak. I went to a lawyer to get a divorce and was in the process of filing when Mubarak called. He told me to wait for him a while longer and everything would be okay. Well, it didn't look like it would be okay to me at the time, so I continued the process of getting a divorce which was going to take some time. In the meantime, I worked the graveyard shift in patient accounts at the hospital in town and was having a hard time finding any future in that. Teachers were a tradition in our family, and I did know that I loved children so is that the way I should go? Although my mom was a teacher and now an administrator, she never did push me in that direction. I really did enjoy helping her and working with students in her classroom though, when I was in high school.

Anyway, one day an old boyfriend heard that I was in town and called me. Naturally, he was the one that I always wanted to marry, but he went off to college when I was sixteen, and I rarely saw him anymore except for a few letters here and there. He would pop in and see me a few times and that was about it.

He did come to visit me, and I found that I was still attracted to him. However, I noticed that his mind seemed preoccupied at times just like before. He still seemed to just want to pop in on me when it suited him, and I had a feeling that he was seeing someone else anyway.

I went out to eat with some girlfriends one day and saw him at the restaurant. I got up to get our pizza, and he immediately walked over to me. He said hi, and we talked for a short while. Suddenly he whispered in my ear saying that one of the biggest mistakes that he made in his life was not marrying me. Then he abruptly walked away. I was shocked to say the least. I didn't know whether to laugh or cry. What was that all about, and then he walked away? After his little game of playing hard to get, I found it hard to believe that he would have married me. I just stood there for a moment thinking, "Why did he just say that and walk away?"

I never saw him again after that, and he didn't contact me again. I called him at home a couple of times, but no one answered the phone. I wanted to see if there really was any hope for us before I made the decision to return to Saudi Arabia again.

Unfortunately, I didn't have the chance to talk to him again about his actions because the following week, Mubarak called and said that he was free and going to fly to Florida. He was going to send me a plane ticket to meet him there.

Why Florida when he was in Houston? Who was in Florida that he knew? Since I was still stupidly in love with him, I went. After all, he still was my husband "till death do us part" or so I thought at the time. The divorce never did go through partly because I don't think that I was ready to end our relationship just yet. When I arrived in Florida, he was standing at the airport waiting for me. We stayed in Florida with some of his friends for about a week and then left for Yemen. He said he was very sorry about everything. Was he?

11. Back to Yemen

Why in the world did we have to go back to Yemen of all the places in the world? Mubarak explained that we would go to Riyadh as soon as he could get us an entry visa to Saudi Arabia. It had to come through Yemen because he was born in Yemen and was never made a Saudi Citizen. We had to wait in Yemen again not knowing how long it would take.

When we arrived in Yemen, this time, I was glad that I knew some Arabic. It didn't feel like such a strange place. First we stayed in a hotel, and for some reason I wasn't feeling very good. The food that the hotel made was very spicy. They must have thrown in about ten jalapeno peppers with curry in everything that they cooked. Mubarak wouldn't let me leave the hotel, so I went up on the roof to take walks and lay out in the sun. The hotels and houses had patios to walk around on and view the entire city. Now that I think about it, I was fortunate that somebody didn't kidnap or kill me for laying out on the roof in my swimsuit. That was not a smart thing to do, and I wonder why Mubarak allowed it. Finally, just when I was about to lose my mind being locked up in the hotel, Mubarak said that he found a house that we could move into immediately.

The next morning one of his friends picked us up and took us to the house. It was a huge house with two living rooms, four bedrooms, three bathrooms, and it included a huge backyard with lizards running around in it. I had never seen lizards that big in my life, and they changed colors right in front of my eyes. They were an ocean blue then suddenly changed to a light green and then dark green. They were truly beautiful and ugly at the same time. Mubarak told me to stay away from them because they spit poison and bite humans. Oh wonderful!

I was still feeling nauseated when an old lady came to visit. She had long, white hair, was bent over, and was wearing an old, ragged dress. She looked like the old witch in the Disney movie Snow White. She had brought some food for us. It was rice, of course, and chicken with a salad. She was very scary looking, and I wondered if she was one of the people around here who worshipped rocks. Mubarak told me that most of the people were Muslims, but some people worshipped rocks and plants. Why anybody would want to pray to a rock is beyond me. Did rocks have strange powers that I didn't know about? I felt as though I was being pulled into some of the ancient past of Yemen. There were a lot of strange people around there or was I the strange one? She told me to lie down. She felt my abdomen and said that I was about three weeks pregnant. That explained why I was feeling like I was going to vomit and did so on a regular basis. I asked Mubarak how she could possibly know exactly how many weeks pregnant that I was. He said that it was magic, and she just knew. I thought that sounded creepy. Mubarak made it sound like she really was a witch, so I was getting worried about eating the food that she brought us. He said she knew that I was an American, and she might have put a spell on the food. As ancient as this country was I sort of believed she might very well know how to use black magic or have some kind of power, but I was hungry so I ate the food. Maybe I shouldn't have. I never did have much good luck come my way after I ate that food or was that Mubarak telling me that, and I was dumb enough to believe him.

We didn't have much food to eat. I'm sure Mubarak just wanted to go home to his family in Riyadh. He purchased very little food at the market. We ate a lot of spaghetti with tuna that was actually pretty good. It was cooked with onions in olive oil, green peppers, and hot peppers, tomato paste, and tuna and finally the spaghetti was mixed in with the sauce.

After several weeks the visa still hadn't arrived, so it didn't look hopeful that we would be leaving soon. He went to work for one of his friends in a doctor's office. The days were long and lonely when he left at eight in the morning and didn't come back until ten at night. I tried to keep busy cleaning or wandering around the house. One day I decided to go into a small room that had a lock on it, but to my surprise it opened. I found boxes and boxes of women's clothes. They were beautiful Arabian clothes made of silk and all kinds of designs. In my boredom, I decided to try some on and they actually fit.

Well, at least I found something else to do for awhile. Mubarak said the clothes were left from the people who lived there before, and they weren't coming back. The owner said I could have the clothes if I wanted them. I often wondered why those people weren't coming back. This house gave me a creepy feeling too, but maybe that was because it always felt so cold inside. The marble floors were always so cool and the lights in the house were very dim. My imagination was going somewhere again, and I needed to bring myself back to reality.

A month went by and no sign of the visa. Mubarak took me to an Egyptian doctor, and sure enough I was pregnant. That was happy news. I just wished the vomiting would stop. Mubarak brought some lamb and vegetables home one day, so I made a stew which was nice because I was getting dreadfully tired of eating tuna and spaghetti. The smell of tuna right now was making me nauseous.

One morning I decided to go out into the yard and lay out in the sun because without a television and lack of books to read I was feeling extremely lonely and bored. Then the weirdest thing happened. There were five huge lizards that kept coming closer to me while several huge black hawks started flying in circles right over my head. They started swooping in a circle closer and closer to the ground and swarming around me. Their actions frightened me such that I ran into the house and shut the door. Well, so much for lying out and getting some sun. Now I was stuck in the house again. That night I told Mubarak about what happened. He just laughed, and said that I'd better be careful and keep my eyes open. He said that there were also wild dogs and packs of wolves wandering around as well and warned me not to open the door to the street.

That was another thing that was interesting. There were stone walls all around the house, and they went up about thirty or more feet high. Mubarak said it was for privacy, and the women could walk outside around the house without any men seeing them. To me it was like being in a jail. Furthermore, I don't know how these women survived not being able to see anything because of walls all around them and not being allowed to go out to the store or anywhere unless their husbands would take them. If the husband is grouchy, a woman could be stuck alone in the house for weeks. I couldn't believe that he wouldn't take me anywhere. This situation was really making me angry, to say the least. Being pregnant and grouchy in a foreign country is not good, especially having to deal with a hole in the floor for a toilet. Let me tell you it is not easy to squat when one is pregnant. I was just thankful not to have seen any of those yellow poisonous scorpions in the bathroom at night. Although, a number of times there were huge black spiders that would crawl over my feet as I walked to the bathroom during the night. They were at least three inches long and as wide. They never came into the bed though. Thank goodness!

That night after my little ordeal with the birds and lizards, Mubarak brought some of his friends to the house and actually let me sit in the living room with them. It was nice to be able to talk to some other people even though only one of them could speak English really well. That was because he had gone to school in England. His name was Waleed, and his friend's name was Khalid. Khalid was very nice and tall. I never ever met an Arabian as tall as he was ever again. He had to be about six foot four. I knew this because my dad was six foot four. I think he was the tallest man in Yemen. He said that he worked for the government, so he always carried a gun and a Yemeni knife. He evidently helped with security. The tradition of Yemen was that if anyone would pull out the knife, he would have to strike blood during a fight. They still follow that practice today. Khalid did take his knife out and show it to me, but he said that he didn't want my blood. "Not funny," I said. Mubarak and Waleed had to translate what Khalid was saying since his English was not very proficient. He knew a few words and seemed to want to learn more English. Every time he came to visit he would say the new word that I had taught him. I told him that was wonderful that he remembered those words. After a couple of months I'm proud to say that I could actually talk to him in English. That's when I decided I would love to teach foreigner's English. He was so proud of himself when he spoke the English language. Khalid and Waleed became very good friends and seemingly liked Americans.

Khalid was very respectable toward me. He was a true Yemeni who had never left his country. He told me that if I ever needed help and ever tired of Mubarak that he would be there for me and respected Americans very much after meeting me. He said that he would never believe any bad things about Americans ever again or in the future. This made me feel good to hear an Arab say something good about my country. I decided that if I was pregnant with a boy that I would name my son Khalid because this Khalid was so good to me. Khalid also means strength and courage in Arabic. My son would definitely need this living in such an aggressive environment and country. Mubarak would of course approve since this was an Arabic name. I would give him a nickname Kelly for short in the American culture, so I would have both names with which I was very satisfied. I knew my parents would like the name Kelly, which of course they did.

Every night Waleed and Khalid would sit with us and bring bags of several branches with huge green leaves on them. They would chew the leaves. I recognized it, from when I was a flight attendant, as khat. They would put one leaf at a time in their mouth, chew it for awhile, and then let it sit in their cheek. They would then eat another leaf and do the same thing. They told me to try it which I did. It tasted awful causing me to spit it out after chewing on it for a minute or so. They said it made them feel good. It just made me sick, but if they liked eating leaves I guess that was their choice. I told them that I would pass on the leaves. It actually tasted like a leaf from an Oak tree that I remember tasting as a child when I was doing the dare game with my friends. They continued talking and eating leaves until about two in the morning. I played cards with Mubarak while they talked. I soon tired of their chatter and decided that it was time to go to bed.

Each night as I climbed into to bed, the wolves started howling, and the dogs would begin barking. It seemed they were getting closer and closer when a huge, black spider ran over my foot. As I looked around to see if there were more spiders hanging around, my eyes focused on one of the plentiful scorpions that lived in Yemen. (Here we go again.) I decided that it was no use to be afraid of their antics, so I got up and killed the scorpion and the spider. I wasn't ready to die yet. I was braver now than on my first trip to Yemen. As I mentioned briefly before I did some research and found out that these scorpions were one of the world's most dangerous ones that contained highly potent venom. Many deaths were reported every year because of bites from these creatures. This particular breed of scorpion is called the Leiurus quinquestriatus. They are said to come out at night from the desert and are said to be found in cracks in the walls of buildings made of stone and bricks. I noticed them on several occasions in the bathroom at night as they crawled from the cracks in the stone walls. This is one thing that Mubarak did tell me the truth about. The yellow and black scorpions manifested the most toxins and could cause severe shock in their victims. I was soon going to see these huge, black scorpions when I moved to Saudi Arabia.

I pleaded with Mubarak to start working on the entry visa's to get into Riyadh. I didn't want to have a baby in this God forsaken country out in the middle of nowhere without any good doctors that we knew of.

We also didn't have any food to eat except tuna, spaghetti, and eggs. There were a few markets to obtain food but few shops or souks to buy clothes or other items. Oddly enough, the next week we both got our entry visas, and Mubarak tried to get us tickets to get out of Yemen. Hopefully, I would never have to come back here again. Since I knew that Riyadh was a big city and that his family was there, I hoped our lives would be better this time around. Surely we could have a better life in Riyadh, and there would be more opportunities for the both of us.

12. Living with His Parents

*I*t was supposed to be a two hour flight to Riyadh, but it was turning out to be a lot longer than that. We had to go to Jeddah first because there was an emergency with the plane. We had to get off. Of course, I didn't have a visa to stay there. As a result, there soon appeared four military men with guns and, naturally, they pointed them at me and told me that I had to spend the night in the airport jail. I told them in Arabic to quit pointing their guns at me because I wasn't a criminal. Mubarak told me not to talk back to them. I replied to Mubarak and the officers, "Well, it isn't my fault that the plane had something go wrong, now was it?" They didn't like my retort and pushed me toward the jail. Mubarak sat outside of the jail while I went inside to a huge room that was blocked off with guards surrounding it. The women were to go inside while the men were somewhere else. I never did understand why Mubarak got to sit outside. There was a huge orange couch in the back of the room where they kept me, so I went back there to lie down for the night. It seemed strange that there was a couch to lie on in the airport jail. I never have seen a bright orange couch like this one in my life. It was as colorful as a pumpkin.

We couldn't get a flight out until the next afternoon. I just hoped that those guards would leave me alone because Mubarak wasn't able to help me in this situation. He had to do what they told him to do. Finally, I dozed for a couple of hours. I had been more tired than I thought. When it was time for our flight the next day, the guard said something in Arabic and motioned with his gun for me to get out of the room.

Finally, we were back on the plane, and it was one of those flights with all the branches and leaves everywhere on the floor. At least I knew what they were and why they were all over the floor. At this point I was so tired I didn't care that I had to walk over all of the greenery and the fact that the plane was so packed, and hot, and noisy. I just wanted to get to Riyadh.

The plane made two more stops. My guess was that we were flying during the time of year of the Hajj, (when the Muslims make their Pilgrimage to Mecca). After we arrived in Riyadh I had to cover with the black cape and black scarf before getting off the plane. Mubarak said that he would be getting me a veil because it was the law to wear it with the (black cape) abiyah. Since I was American I should be okay walking around without it for the time being.

His brother was at the airport waiting to take us to his parent's house. By this time they were living in a different place than our last visit. The airport was about an hour away from where they lived. As we neared their home, I noticed that the roads were unpaved and were just dirt pathways. The house was surrounded with the huge walls that made me feel like I was in a jail all the time. I was reminded again that women must be secluded so that other men couldn't see them. It was a big house and much better looking than their other house. We walked up two flights of stairs and went into the living room where his mom, dad, sisters, and brothers greeted us. They seemed very happy to see us which made us both feel better to be back. We sat down to talk and drink some customary tea (shohee). His parents killed a lamb for us, which was the tradition when a family returns from a long trip.

The meal consisted of lamb and rice with a salad, as usual. We also enjoyed fresh dates and homemade cake. I had almost forgotten what lamb tasted like, but as I remembered, Mubarak's mom was a very good cook. The lamb had a really different taste than beef. It had more of a wild, strong taste almost like my first taste of venison. We all stayed up late that night talking and drinking more shohee (hot tea). When we went upstairs to bed, I noticed that we had a much larger room than in the other house! It was on the roof, which was difficult for me to adjust to. The roof was also used as a play area for soccer because there was a huge concreted area surrounded by walls that made it safe for the children as well as the women.

Mubarak was much more content in Riyadh. This did help our relationship, and we both felt much safer living with his parents.

The next morning the entire family had a large breakfast of eggs, a bean dish, feta cheese, jelly, hummus, and other dips for bread. Bread and dip were served at each meal. My guess was that the bread was used as filler so less meat or other foods were needed.

I discovered the reason that Mubarak tried so hard to get back home was because it was the month of Ramadan. Ramadan is one of the most important times of the year for Muslims. It's like Christmas everyday except that you can't eat until the sun goes down. Everybody stays up very late, and the stores don't open until ten at night. The men have their dinner at eight–thirty or so and go to work at nine or ten in the evening. They don't come back home from work until two in the morning to have their supper.

The women start cooking at noon to make the breakfast that's eaten when the sun goes down at five or six in the evening. They break their fast by eating dates and drinking Arabic coffee because these were the traditions of the Prophet Muhammad. The traditions of the Prophet Muhammad were strictly followed.

The Arabic coffee is very bitter, so the dates help it tremendously. They also drink grape juice. It's made from a kind of syrup. The juice was always served without ice. I asked Mubarak, "Why doesn't anybody ever put ice in their drinks? It would be nice to have a cold icy drink in such a hot country." He told me that it's not good for a person's throat. It's too cold with the dry desert atmosphere. I told him that I thought it was a very silly notion and didn't make much sense. Our conversations would usually go back and forth about certain senseless subjects like ice until finally Mubarak would say, "Give it up because this is just our way." He said that there's no way that I could change the people. However, I noticed the younger generation seemed to be very open minded and willing to change.

They also eat soup after they break their fast. It is usually made with lamb. Oatmeal is put into the lamb broth with the lamb, and lemons are then squeezed into the soup. This was very satisfying and healthy after fasting all day. Samboosa is also eaten with the soup. This is mutton cooked with onions, mint, parsley leaves, and different spices. Then it is rolled up into a triangle with phyllo dough and finally dropped into hot oil. After breaking their fast everybody gets up to pray.

The men go to the mosque, and the women pray at home. The men as well as the women lay a small beautifully designed silk rug on the floor and pray on top of it. Most of the rugs that I have seen have a picture of a mosque on them which can be bought in many different colors. I wanted to go to the mosque to pray, but Mubarak said that it was better for me to pray at home. He then stated that the prophet Muhammad is said to have proclaimed, as one of the hadiths, (sayings of the prophet) that, "The woman is nearest to her Lord's face when she is in the innermost part of her home. Her prayer in the courtyard of her house, and her prayer in her chamber is even better than her prayer in her home." Mubarak also told me that the prophet Muhammad said that if a woman leaves the house without her husband's permission, the angels curse her till she comes back to his house or repents. I decided to stay at home and pray after I fasted because I didn't want to be cursed by the angels all night. Of course, I couldn't decide yet if I should believe all of that, but who knows living in one of the most ancient countries in the world what could happen.

Mubarak said that next to the Holy Quran, the Hadith is the second source that should be abided by in connection with the Islamic law that is related to one's social and personal behavior, because the commandments of the Prophet Muhammad are as obligatory to the believers as the commandments of Allah.

During Ramadan the main meal is eaten two or more hours after breakfast and consists of lamb or chicken served with rice or other types of stews. After this meal the men sometimes take naps and then go to work until two in the morning. The women go shopping or visit their neighbors. At this time of year the women like to take food to each others' houses and sit and talk until midnight. Then they start making supper. It took me awhile to get used to cooking so late at night. Everybody eats the late supper and stays up until the next prayer right before sunrise, and finally, everyone goes to bed. Ramadan lasts about thirty days then everyone celebrates for a couple of days afterward.

During Ramadan many women are seen shopping at the malls in the city of Riyadh more than any other time of the year that I noticed.

The shopping malls are huge and similar to the ones in the United States. There are many high fashion name brands. Numerous stores sell gold that the women love to buy.

I was just happy to be out of the house and to be able to walk around a mall even though I did have to completely cover my body and face with the black garments. I unfortunately always seemed to get into trouble by the Mutaween. These were the religious police who enforced the rules of Islam. They have authority over the citizens as well as visitors of the country. They had the authority to order floggings, imprisonment and public humiliation. Anyone who was doing something that wasn't the Islamic way of life would be in dire trouble. Listening to American music they called rock and roll was forbidden and would be a reason for punishment. Mubarak called them Mutawahs (the Islamic priests) or radical Islamists.

I needed to uncover my eyes so I could see where I was going, or I would trip over my cape and fall. I never did know how the Arabic women could see through those veils. When I asked they would tell me that they had to, or they could be put in jail. So far I had been lucky that nobody wanted to put me in jail yet because I was always ready to fight with these strange and heartless men, and, I didn't like being yelled at or hit with a stick because I needed to see where I was going.

After the approximate thirty day period of Ramadan, Eid begins, and all the families get together to visit and have huge feasts just like on our holidays except for different religious reasons. They celebrate that their fasting time is over for the year. The night before Eid the women put henna on their hands. Henna is from a plant. It is a dry powder mixed with water and lemon. It has a very strong smell and looks like mud with an orange hue. It is often used on the hair as well. I remember that my mother used to use it sometimes to give her dark brown hair a reddish hue. Mubarak's sister Fatima would leave it on her hair all night. On the morning of Eid she would wash it off. It made reddish highlights that were very beautiful mixed in her black hair. Mubarak's sister Jameliah would decorate my hands with floral or other designs using the henna. It took eight hours or more before it dried. After washing the dried henna off it looks like tattoos on one's hands. It leaves an orange colored design on the hands. Henna is also used for weddings. It is called "The Night of the Henna" the night before the wedding day. It is the custom for the bride and family to wear henna on their hands for the wedding day. They also put it on their feet and ankles. After three months or so it fades away.

Also, on the morning of the Eid everybody wears new clothes, and the girls put on their new dresses and new shoes. Even the men and boys wear their newest white robes made by a tailor specifically for this day. It reminded me a bit of Easter seeing all the little girls wearing new colorful dresses. For lunch or dinner families have a big feast at home and later go to the fair, parks, or to the desert for picnics. This celebration lasts for three or four days.

By this time I could speak and understand Arabic better which really helped me in conversing with the Arabic women. I found that they had a very good sense of humor. It seemed to me that it was their saving grace since they were so confined. Mubarak's mother (Barka) said that when she gets any money from her sons or husband, she hides it. She said it's very hard not having any money and not being able to work. Barka's mother was part Indian and came from India. Barka rarely gets to visit her home in India and misses it terribly. She doesn't have to wear the black cape in India but does wear the various Sari's that are made of many beautiful colors of material. The one time that she went to India while I was living there Barka brought me a Sari from India, and Mubarak's sisters taught me how to dance Hindi. The Sari's are very colorful. Mine was red with gold sequins and gold designs embroidered all over. The Indians also cover their hair but with beautifully colored scarves that match their clothes. Barka and her daughters would watch Hindi movies, and I would watch with them. I learned a few words in Hindi, but I wanted to master the Arabic language since that was what my husband spoke. "There are movie theaters and other entertainment in India, not like Riyadh," Barka told me. I really missed going to see a movie, but it was against the law to have movie theaters in Riyadh.

Another problem, according to Mubarak's sisters, is the driving situation in Riyadh. They feel very upset that they can't drive but know if they try they would be killed or put in jail. Fortunately, his sisters were very diligent with their studies. They loved going to school. Of course, there really isn't much else to do there but study, cook, and visit with other girls and women at social gatherings.

After Ramadan, the season began to change to the summer and the desert heat was unbearable, especially when one was pregnant. The temperature frequently reached one hundred and thirty degrees Fahrenheit.

Children were told to stay inside after about eleven in the morning because it was so hot. Some homes had air conditioners that were installed into the walls, but the rooms still remained warm even at the high setting. The days were long and hot.

When I awakened in the morning, I would sit on the kitchen floor with the women and help or watch them prepare the day's meals. There were so many girls in the kitchen that they didn't really need much more help, but I watched and learned how to cook Arabic food. They incorporate a variety of spices and hot peppers into their recipes. I began to enjoy the food they made. I really liked the salad. They would sit on the floor and chop the vegetables for hours. They would chop lettuce, carrots, tomatoes, and cucumbers in small square pieces. Then pour olive oil over the salad, add salt, pepper, cumin, and then squeeze lemon on top. (I like it better without the cumin in it.) That was how they made their salad dressing which is probably a lot healthier than some of our American dressings. Now that I look back, that was probably the healthiest food that I have ever eaten compared to fried chicken, French fries, and onion rings, which is what my American husband Tim, would eat everyday if he could. The chicken and rice dish (kupsa) or lamb and rice were usually made on the weekends. The recipe for that is: cook one medium onion, two or three cloves of garlic in olive oil. Two or three tomatoes can be added for a variation. Add one chicken cut into pieces. Next, add the spices that are: salt, pepper, cumin, curry, turmeric, allspice, peppermint, and parsley. I add half a teaspoon or more of each of these depending on how spicy I want it. Add a hot pepper or two also depending on how hot one wants it. Or it can be omitted. Cook all of this for a few minutes in the oil. Then add enough water to cook the chicken for about an hour or so, and add the rice. Two dried lemons and one or two cinnamon sticks are also added after adding the water. Let the chicken cook for an hour or so until done, and add the rice. I use Basmati rice which does well with this dish, but any other desired rice should work well, too. This chicken dish is always served with the salad. The lamb and rice can be made the same way in one big pot. The Arabs eat this kupsa meal with their hands.

I was usually kept occupied with Mubarak's sisters and relatives most of my days. I never did really know where Mubarak was half the time. He said that he was doing some construction work. One day he came home really late at night, his head was bald, and his face looked like it had been burned. He said he was doing construction work, and a fire broke out that caught his hair and clothes caught on fire. Well, I was relieved that he made it back alive, since being nine months pregnant having the baby alone in Arabia would have been a nightmare. He said that he wasn't going to go back to that job anymore; therefore, we were going to have to keep living with his family. We did have a nice private room to live in though, for which I was thankful. However, I didn't want to live on a roof forever. Further, I did not appreciate being electrically shocked every time I wanted to wash my hands and face either. I was a bit afraid that it might affect the baby, and it was "driving me nuts." He kept telling me that he was going to fix the wires in the bathroom, but he never did.

A picnic at the Saudi desert with Mubarak's family. I'm the tall one in the middle wearing the black cape.

13. Khalid

Shortly thereafter on one of the hottest October nights, I went into labor. Temperatures sometimes reached a hundred and twenty degrees Fahrenheit even during the fall. Mubarak took me to the hospital, and my Jordanian doctor said that I should come back later because I wasn't ready yet. It was nine at night, and it took until nine o'clock the next night before Khalid was born. I decided to call him Khalid because it meant strength, and he would need a lot of that living in the Middle East. Since his American name would be Kelly, it would be an easier adaptation for him when we visited my family in the United States.

It was pretty horrible having a baby without any medication or anything for the pain. I was begging for an aspirin, or anything for that matter, toward the end.

I realize how ridiculous I must have sounded as I don't think that any amount of aspirin would have helped that incredible pain. In the Middle East the women are expected to deliver by a natural birth. However, the nurse said that I could have some hot tea. (Here we go with the shohee again.) The nurse said that it would give me strength, and it must have because after three pushes Khalid came out crying. Fortunately, they did let me hold him right away. He was beautiful of course with the dark, beautiful, olive skin that he still has today. I was relieved in a way that it was a boy because the men like it better when a boy is born first. I also knew that this was a man's world, and it would be nice to have a son that could be with me in the future and allow me the freedom to leave the country if I needed him to get me out.

The next morning Mubarak took us back home, and of course everyone was very happy to see the new baby. A lamb was killed in honor of the baby, and there was a big feast that included more than a hundred people who came to see Khalid. I went upstairs to rest, and one of the girls brought Khalid up later on. This was the happiest moment of my life. I only wished that my mom and the rest of my family could have been with me, but I knew this was how it was going to be. I had to make it alone without my family.

Later on the same week, Jameliah and Fatima came to my room and asked if they could take Khalid downstairs to hold him for awhile. They told me to get some rest, and they would take care of him. When they brought him to me later I saw that his hair was completely gone. I was shocked to see that they had shaved his head. I told Mubarak they should have asked me if they could do that. He said that it was their custom. It was better for new hair to come out because the other hair originated when he was in my womb. I was upset about this strange custom, so I went downstairs and told his mom not to do anything to the baby unless she tells me first. She just laughed, and said, "This is better for him. He will get his beautiful hair back soon." I knew that his hair would grow back, of course. I surmised that she would do what she wanted to do while I was living in her house anyway, so I might as well keep my mouth shut. I soon got over it. Barka was very nice as usual, but there were many times I wondered what she thought of me or said behind my back. Later on I came to find out that she practiced black magic when she traveled to India. She would put a spell on someone whom she didn't like. My son later told me that she had been using her black magic on me.

14. Arabian Neighbor

$\mathcal{M}$ ubarak finally found a good job after Khalid was born. Shortly thereafter, we moved to an apartment. It looked clean, but it was very far away from the city. There wasn't any carpet, so Mubarak said that he would buy some. Naturally, I was expected to lay the carpet while he was at work. The next day he brought me some glue, scissors, a carpet cutter, and the carpet. Khalid just sat in his walker and stared at me while I rolled out the carpet, cut it, and glued it to the floor. He must have been amused watching me because he never cried or said a word while I worked. By the time I was finished, I had blisters all over my hands because there was so much carpet that needed cutting. Since this was my first experience at this, I was really proud of myself for being able to accomplish such a feat. Mubarak said that I did a good job. We never did get a couch to sit on in that apartment until I started working and demanded a couch to buy with the money I earned. In the meantime he bought cushions that were placed along the walls, and we had to sit on the floor because that was the Arabic custom. This tradition was one of the "Hadiths" of the Prophet Muhammad or one of the beliefs that the prophet practiced, so the people imitated his actions.

Mubarak brought camel meat home one night for me to fix for the evening meal. He told me to boil it and throw some rice in with it. Well, it didn't taste very good, so I told him not to bring anymore camel home. I didn't like the idea of eating this strong wild-tasting camel meat although I'm sure many people like it. I decided that I would much rather watch them run around in the desert than eat them.

During the day, while Mubarak was working, my neighbors came to visit. They were very friendly and usually brought some good food. One lady who came to visit was from Africa. She was very tall and wore a turban on her head made of different colors. She made a spicy meat dish which was hot, but delicious. I was getting used to all the spicy dishes and hot peppers by now. She didn't know any English but was able to speak enough Arabic to communicate fairly well. She told me that there were huge rats near the bathroom window and told me not to open it. Now I knew what that noise was that I had been hearing every so often. I'm glad I didn't open that window because I hate rats since I was bitten by one when I was only five years old. The neighbor boy, who was a couple of years older than me, dared me to pick up the rat. I was too young to know better, so I picked it up by its tail whereupon it turned around and bit me. It was a huge rat that looked more like a squirrel. My mom said that I might have to have rabies shots in my stomach if it was sick. Fortunately, for me that never happened. Needless to say, after that incident, I never picked up another wild animal with teeth.

After finding out about the rats, I hoped that we didn't have to live in this apartment too long. My guess was that's what was chewing on our telephone wire. Mubarak kept asking why I was cutting our telephone wire. I told him, "Why in the world would I do that because that's my only link to the outside world."

Then one night he brought a cage home and caught a huge, gray, ugly rat that was as big as a possum. I said, "Now what are you going to do with it?" He said he was going to pour boiling water on it to kill it. I wondered where the Arabian men folk get all their ideas to torture animals. I told him that I wasn't going to watch him do it. He left the cage with the dead ammonia smelling rat on the sink for me to see. It was stiff and horrible looking from having boiled water poured on it. I felt sorry that it had to die that way, but I was glad that it couldn't run around our house anymore and chew up the wires. Mubarak told me to be sure to keep the bathroom windows closed.

My other neighbor, whose name was Fatima was from Jeddah, Saudi Arabia. She and her husband were very religious. Fatima would come over everyday to help me with my conversational Arabic. She was anxious for me to learn about Islam and how to read the Qur'an. She said that it was her duty as a Muslim to teach me about Islam. I had to learn to read the Qur'an from right to left because that's how all Arabic is read. She taught me that Islam was the religion of Saudi Arabia, and everyone must abide by its rules. There were five pillars of Islam: First of all, Muslims must believe there is only one God (Allah). Recitation of this verse in Arabic is mandatory for one to become a Muslim. The second part is Iqamat-as-Salat: In English the priest says, "Come to pray, come to pray, it is best for you if you only knew." This second part is a warning to pray five times a day. There is a loud, eerie call to prayer on a loudspeaker by the priest in the mosque. It is so loud that it can be heard throughout the town and even in people's homes. The five calls to prayer occur at sunrise, noon, late afternoon, sunset, and during the darkest part of the night, at approximately eight or nine o'clock. Men are required to pray at the mosque, but women are allowed to pray at home. The third rule is to pay Zakat. Zakat is a certain amount of money paid yearly to the poor in the Muslim community, and food is also given as Zakat. A large bag of rice for a poor family would be one sufficient way of paying the Zakat. This sounds a bit like what we Christians try to do as we donate to various charities or church charity needs. The fourth rule of Islam is to perform Hajj. Hajj is a pilgrimage to the (Kabah) house in Mecca required once in a lifetime by every Muslim who can afford the expenses and is physically able. Performing Hajj eliminates all previous sins and gives admittance to the doors of paradise. The final rule is (Saum) that requires fasting during the month of Ramadan. All Muslims must abstain from food or any liquids from sunrise to sunset during this time. After sunset the Muslims break their fast with Arabic coffee and dates. This is how the prophet Muhammad broke his fast, so the Muslims do the same. A Muslim must persevere in all five rules (or parts) to succeed in Islam. If a person renounces Islam, he or she will be beheaded.

I definitely learned a lot about Islam from Fatima. The sayings from the Prophet Muhammad are called Hadiths which are also laws that should be abided by every Muslim as well. She also told me that women must cover their bodies and wear a veil. It sounds like this was also from the Prophet Muhammad who demanded his wives be covered with a veil so other men couldn't see them.

Covering with a veil is supposed to protect the women, and keep other men from looking at them. However, after living in the Middle East for almost fourteen years, I observed that if a Saudi man wants to be with somebody, he will figure out a way to do it. One way that the women meet men is to give notes to them or have somebody else do it. This sounds like what my girlfriends and I did in high school. (Later, my son told me that this is what he did when he wanted to meet a girl.)

Our first apartment

My view from the kitchen window.

15. Jinns

As the months passed Khalid learned to sit and soon learned to walk backwards in his walker. One day a bad storm threatened, and he walked himself to a room with a small patio. I wasn't allowed on the patio because women weren't supposed to be seen. The door didn't latch correctly. Anyway, I went into the kitchen for a minute and heard the door slam shut and lock. He had walked to the door and pushed himself outside with his walker. It took all my strength to push the door open only to experience hail, as big as a baseball, flying into my face and into the room. As I grabbed Khalid the door slammed shut again, and I couldn't get it open. I covered Khalid as the hail continued to pelt my back and face. I had never seen hail that big back home in Indiana. With a lot of effort I finally got the door open again.

When Mubarak came home that night, I explained to him what happened. His response was that there were probably jinns around. I hadn't heard that before and asked him what they were. He told me that they were demons and that we were living on the horns of the devil- whatever that meant. I really didn't want to know, but strange and creepy things did seem to happen around here. He went to check the doors. He said that they were okay, but he did try to make sure that it didn't lock on its own again. He said the wind that came in must have sucked the door tight. I wish he wouldn't have told me about the jinns because it made me think about them since I was usually alone in the apartment. He told me to pray to God so they would go away, hopefully. Then he started laughing.

Well, the next day Khalid got himself in a real jam again. He got his finger smashed in a door while he was snooping around the apartment in his little walker. Unfortunately, we still didn't have a phone because of the rat chewing all the wires, and Mubarak never did tell me his work number. I could tell by looking at his finger that Khalid needed to get stitches. There was a lot of blood, and he was screaming. I threw my black cape and veil on and went out the door carrying my screaming little, beautiful baby.

The neighbors weren't answering their doors, so I had to walk to Mubarak's parent's house and hoped that I could remember how to get there. I presumed it was about two miles away. Fortunately, I did remember where I was going, but it was really creepy and deserted on the streets, and I was beginning to wonder why. Women didn't normally go out walking alone. Here I was out on the street hoping that I wouldn't be noticed. I was thankful that it was such a cloudy day because wearing my black cape when the sun was beating down at a hundred and thirty degrees was a nightmare. It seemed like an eternity until I arrived at Barka's and nobody was coming to answer the door. I waited for ten or fifteen minutes and finally Mubarak's older brother Omar answered the door and took Khalid and me straight to the doctor. I was right about his finger. The doctor did have to stitch the finger. Khalid didn't like it, but I sure was glad that I ventured out into those deserted streets to save his finger. After that little incident, I told Mubarak that we really needed to have a phone so that I could call him in case of an emergency. He didn't reply, so I guess he just figured that nothing else would happen to us. That was when I was beginning to worry about being alone with Khalid in a foreign country, and for the first time in my life I was starting to feel really helpless.

Khalid and me-henna on my hands

Khalid and me at a park

Korean Embassy School

16. The Korean Embassy School

One day I asked Mubarak for permission to get a job. Surprisingly he consented. I met a woman who said that The Korean Embassy School was looking for an American to teach the children English. The Principal interviewed me, and I was hired to teach at the Embassy. Since I wasn't allowed to drive, Mubarak hired a man from the Philippines to take me back and forth to school everyday. I didn't know Korean, but Mr. Lee, the principal at the time, said that he only wanted me to speak English in class. The students knew very little English, but they were quick learners. I used a lot of visuals on most of their worksheets as I was teaching a lesson. I had to make my own drawings most of the time or cut and paste out pictures and copy them. It seemed to really help them remember words when they could visualize them. Sometimes I would stay in the room with the Korean teachers and watch the students write. They had to learn to write Chinese which looked as difficult as Arabic to me. The teachers said that the students had to get used to learning more than one language. I thought it was interesting that it was mandatory for the Korean children to learn more than one language at such an early age.

Later on I tried to learn how to speak some words in Korean and learn what types of food they eat. I learned that they eat Kimchee with every meal. (Kimchee is pickled cabbage that is very spicy.) It's really good for one's stomach. I could never eat spicy, cold cabbage at every meal though. My mom would make sauerkraut with ribs which were good, but I wouldn't be able to eat sauerkraut everyday.

At about ten o' clock every morning the teachers would ask me to sit with them and eat what they called a snack that seemed more of a meal to me. They had vegetable sushi and spicy pasta and other kinds of spicy rather doughy foods. It was very good! I felt that I was learning while I was teaching the students and felt extremely lucky to have such a great opportunity to work at their embassy school. I wish I would have been more interested in learning the Korean language at the time, but I was simultaneously trying to become more proficient in Arabic. I discovered that children seem to learn languages much faster than adults.

The children were always so eager to learn English. Once in a while I would put on a sing-along -songs movie. They would love to watch and sing along with the English. Sometimes I was invited to watch them do their Taekwondo in the gym. (Taekwondo is a type of karate.) They could jump as high as the ceiling, and the ones who could do that were only in the fourth grade. They would laugh and tell me to stay and watch them. They loved to show-off when I was around. I was becoming so attached to the children and loved each and every one of them.

I worked at the Korean Embassy for a little over four years. It was one of the most enlightening and informative experiences that I have ever had. The Korean people were polite, educated, and very friendly. I still recall every morning as I walked down the hall every teacher would nod and smile good morning to me, and I did the same. They made you feel at home.

17. The Islamic School

During the time that I was working at the Korean Embassy, I started going to a religious Islamic school at night to learn how to read the Qur'an. I met an American girl from Seattle who had changed her American name to Aiisha. Aiisha was the name of the Prophet Muhammad's wife. She met her husband in the United States, as I did, and came over to Saudi to live. She was one of the few girls whom I knew there who gave up her American name and nationality. Personally, I did not agree with that because I loved my country, and I always will even if I have to again live in another country-heaven forbid. I was always proud to say that I was an American, and I almost got myself killed a couple of times saying it; however, I thought that to stand up for my country was the right thing to do.

Aiisha told me about the school, so I went to check it out to learn more about Islam being as I was very curious why these women were so proud to cover themselves and pray at all times of the day. All I knew was that to wear that black cape and cover my face and head with black material in a hundred and thirty degree temperature seemed on the frigid side of good common sense to me. I thought I was going to pass out most of the time, but I guess it kept my face from getting burned and maybe from getting skin cancer as most of us are worried about nowadays. I just wanted to put on a bikini and lay out in the sun since there was so much of it. Mubarak was not really in favor of my sunbathing and warned me many times to be careful and to make sure that nobody sees me if I go up on the roof, because the men will attack me or kill me. I guess he thought that I'd make the right choice, but he should have known that at times I do things on the spur of the moment and worry about the consequences later.

The Islamic school was interesting for awhile, but I thought that the women were a bit radical or too far "out in left field" for me. I basically wanted to learn how to read the Qur'an in Arabic, but after one of the teachers smacked me on my arm I decided otherwise. The teacher said that I was forbidden to write with my left hand. I couldn't write English with my right hand so how in the world was I supposed to write Arabic. I guess I could have learned to right with my right hand since I also had to eat with my right hand as well, but I was starting to feel this was getting a bit discriminatory.

After she listened to me read the Qur'an she hit me again and said that I was reading too slow. I told her, "How can I possibly read fast when I can hardly read any of the words?" I was surprised to find myself actually reading a whole sentence as I barely had the alphabet memorized at the time. I was irate, to say the least, and abruptly stood up from my chair. I told her that I came to this class searching for a good teacher (not like her) to teach me how to read Arabic and furthermore, she had no right to hit me. She was on the other side of the room and immediately came charging toward me fuming with anger. If she had a gun I'm sure she would have shot me. She stood in front of me and shouted in Arabic for me to get out of her room. She said la Allah el llalah. (There is only one God.) I was a lot bigger and taller than her or most of those women and was thinking to knock the heck out of her but decided not to lower myself to her primitive ways of thinking. I just walked away. She wasn't worth me being put in jail by the Taliban or Mutaween or whatever they called themselves. Later on one of the Arabic women studying at the school told me that the teacher didn't want an American in her class. That was just fine because I would have Mubarak and his sisters teach me how to read and write Arabic. After awhile I did learn how to read Arabic and speak very well due to many close friendships with the more open-minded Arabic women. After that little incident I decided to stay far away from the Muslim extremists. These women didn't even let their eyes show through their veil. I couldn't see when I did that and kept tripping over myself. I really didn't want to fall flat on the ground in the street or break my leg, I had to let my eyes show through and furthermore, I like to wear the black eyeliner under my eyes like the Egyptian women taught me because I thought it looked really cool at the time. Some Arabic women said that would attract the men if I did that. I responded that the men must be really hard up in this country to be attracted to a woman's eyes. Mubarak said my green eyes gave away that I wasn't Saudi. Only the Bedouins had blue eyes, and there were very few of them. He never really made me cover my eyes except when the priests (mutaween) would come by and hit me with a stick or cane and tell me that I was an atheist and a bad woman for letting my eyes show.

One time when I was walking in the shopping mall minding my own business an old man with a long white beard was quickly walking toward me with his long stick. It looked like a long skinny branch off a tree. As he was walking toward me he raised his stick then swatted my leg with it. He said that I shouldn't be wearing jeans nor should I let my eyes be showing. He told me Hurom. (It's a sin.) I was about ready to grab the stick from him and run away with it and yell at him in English, but I didn't because Mubarak said that they would put me in jail and chop my head off. It was crazy that I didn't have the right to speak or say much of anything in Saudi without getting my head chopped off. I wondered how people could live such backward ways and be so angry if a woman's eyes were showing. I guess I really belabor this point, but it really aggravated me and still does.

18. Lina

As time went on I met two other American women through Mubarak's friends. One was married to a Saudi and the other to a Palestinian. Lina was married to the one from Jordon. She was the friendliest and most open-minded. She was originally from Tennessee. She showed me pictures of her dad and said that she had not been able to go back home again. She thought that later on she would be moving to Jordon and live there permanently. She was always getting pregnant and ended up having seven beautiful children by the last time I saw her. The other American girl that I met through Lina was a very strict Muslim, and she gave up her American citizenship for the Saudi nationality. She was nice too, but I think Lina was a little more reasonable and didn't want to give up her nationality at the time. I ended up liking Lina the best. We both grew up in small towns in the country, but I could tell that she didn't want to go back to the States as of that time. I would have liked to live back home in a heartbeat, but I knew in my heart that Mubarak couldn't survive there. He belonged here in Saudi Arabia where his family was located. I wasn't quite sure what I was going to be doing about that in the future, and I didn't want to think about it at the time since I was so happy with my beautiful and energetic two year old son.

One Halloween Lina and I dressed our kids up and went trick-or-treating at a few of our Americans' friends' houses. I don't think that the husbands liked that very much. Together, one night Lina and I even made popcorn balls. It's a wonder we didn't get caught by somebody and get into trouble, but I guess the men were too busy doing other things. They knew what they had gotten into by marrying American women or at least they thought they knew.

19. The Gulf War

One night shortly thereafter, a loud, piercing, eerie siren awakened us from a deep sleep. Only minutes later the American Embassy called and said there were some scud missiles en route to Riyadh that might be loaded with chemicals. We were told to put on our gas masks. I jumped out of bed and grabbed Khalid from his crib then put him down for a minute to get the masks. Mubarak said that he was going to the roof to watch the scud missiles come over. I told him to wait for us, but he was already out the door. Suddenly, Khalid dashed from the bedroom to the living room, and simultaneously, there was a loud sonic boom which caused the entire building to shake. All the windows sounded like they were cracking and going to shatter at any moment. Trembling, I caught Khalid just as he lost his balance and was about to fall backward from the explosion. As I was wondering about Mubarak, I was oblivious that everything became very still. I cautiously walked up to the roof while I was holding onto Khalid with a death grip. I glanced over to see Mubarak standing frozen and looking up into the sky. He said that a Patriot missile just blew the scud missile in half. He described it as looking like The Fourth of July. Just then, we heard another siren. Soon another scud came and was blown up by a patriot missile. It did look like fireworks. I was thankful the scud missile didn't hit our apartment and would have hit us if it weren't for the patriot missile. The remains of the missile landed in a ditch on the other side of our apartment. Of course, we had to be living thirty minutes out of the city where the scuds were dropping first. Later I found out that there was an American military base close by which is why our area was being targeted. Finally, we heard another siren, and Mubarak said that was the all clear sign for the time being. The next morning after Mubarak ventured out he landed upon one intact missile laying down the road by our apartment.

I called home during this episode. Mom and Dad were watching CNN and told us all that was happening. The sirens were blaring one time when I was talking to them. At the same time they were seeing missiles flying into Riyadh on CNN. Over the Arabian television network, Saddam Hussein was making threats to the Saudi Arabian and American bases in the Riyadh area. It was in regard to the Kuwait oil fields-mostly a political situation. Mom suggested that Khalid and I should come home until it was over, but I decided to stay a little longer because of my work. However, after the war started the Korean Embassy was closed.

For the next two weeks the missiles kept coming. Every time the siren went off, my heart skipped a beat, and I immediately grabbed Khalid.

I often asked myself why couldn't I have had a normal life and married somebody from my little hometown because that's all I ever really wanted. Now here I am in a war zone with an Arabian with a possibility of being killed by a scud missile from a madman in Iraq!

When Mubarak went to work in the mornings as usual, I took Khalid up on the roof to get some fresh air and play with his toys while I watched the stealth planes fly over. It was a sight to watch them fly in formation. The stealth planes were black as coal, like bats, and they were alien looking. It gave me the creeps to watch them, but I was glad they were around and that there were American men flying them. It made me feel safe and homesick once again for my own people. The Americans always seemed to be there to help the Arabs, and many of the Saudi citizens had no idea what a real help they were. One of Mubarak's brothers once asked me if we had highways like Saudi Arabia. I replied in Arabic that the Americans were the ones who helped the Arabs build their highways and interstates. That made me crazy that nobody knew what the Americans were doing. They think we are just bad people who want to cause trouble and destroy their religion when that is not true.

The Americans whom I know respect all people and all religions except when we are being attacked, of course, we will fight back.

One day, I noticed there was more dust outside than usual. The sky was getting dark even in the afternoon. This seemed strange. It wasn't like a normal sand storm either. This dust was black as though tiny speckles of coal were falling from the sky. It was getting darker, and the black dust, that seemed sort of oily, was closing in on us. On Impulse, I pulled my scarf over my mouth to keep out the ever thickening black dust. It was getting harder to breathe, so I grabbed Khalid and sprinted downstairs. As I sat down to think about this strange stuff, that darn siren started blaring. Usually it went off at night, but occasionally it would blast off during the day as well. I hated when the sirens went off because there wasn't anywhere to take cover. None of the houses were made with basements like in the United States. I took Khalid and went to the bedroom and put the mattress over our heads. I could only hope this would protect us from any debris that might fly into the room. Khalid would just giggle and was probably thinking it was some sort of game. Khalid was my prince because he always took me into his little world and made me forget about my harsh reality.

Suddenly I heard the door open. It was Mubarak. His immaculately looking white head scarf was covered with the black dust. He walked into our bedroom and said, "You might want to take the American flag down that you have hanging on the wall." I asked why. He said, "Well, we are in a war, and if the Iraqi men see you and the flag hanging there, they are going to kill us." I was actually thinking about that myself, but I so missed my country. That's why I let it hang there.

He asked if I had seen the smoke coming. I said, "Yes," and asked where it was coming from. He said it was from the oil fields in Kuwait. Saddam Hussein was setting them on fire so the Americans couldn't have the oil anymore. I couldn't believe the smoke was traveling so far, but Mubarak said that we were not that far away from Kuwait. He said that all the citizens of Saudi were told to take cover in their houses. We listened to the radio and heard that a scud missile blew up a huge building downtown, and one hit a military base in Dammam. Mubarak reminded me that the reason the scuds kept coming over our apartment was because we were so close to the American military base.

Well, that was just great to hear that the compound was a skip and hop down the street, I decided that I wanted to get out of there and take a short vacation since I couldn't go to work anyhow. All the Koreans left the country and went back home. Maybe it was a good idea for me to leave, too.

I asked Mubarak to get us a ticket to go home, but he said that the airport just closed because there was a threat on the Americans. The planes would probably get blown up on take-off. I then asked him to take us to the military base where I had heard some Americans were leaving on military planes since the airport had closed. Mubarak said that he had talked to an officer who said that Khalid and I needed our American passports then we could leave on a military plane. Unfortunately, the day he was going to take Khalid and me to the military airport, one of the planes had been blown up killing all the civilians aboard. Therefore, they immediately stopped all flights. That was unbelievably scary, and I was glad that we hadn't left on that plane.

After about a week the airport finally opened. Mubarak reserved a flight on American Airlines for me and Khalid to go home. Mubarak said, "Good luck, because the plane might be bombed since it was an American plane." He had heard this from listening to the recent broadcasts coming in from Iraq. Saddam made a threat on all Americans and said that he would blow up any planes coming or leaving. Should I stay, or should I go now?

As I nervously boarded the plane holding Khalid ever so tightly, I pulled off my veil and scarf so I could see where I was going. I took my Abiyah (the black cape) off as well as I shakily walked through the long aisle of the plane. It was a relief to be on an American plane. I refused to believe that the plane would be blown up. It was not going to happen at this time in my life and not with Khalid in my arms. As the plane took off, I prayed to God to put one of his hands out and keep everyone aboard safe. I felt more at peace after my little prayer and gave Khalid a kiss and told him that we were going to go see his Aunt Lisa, Aunt Randa, Grandma, and Grandpa. Amazingly, it was one of the smoothest flights that I had ever flown on.

Khalid next to the American flag

20. Back Home Again

*I*t was a relief to be home and have my freedom again! I was completely free from wearing the traditional Saudi garb. I could put on a pair of jeans and walk down the street without having to worry about being put in jail. I kept telling myself that I needed to make a plan to find a way to live in the USA again.

I came to the conclusion that I would talk to my sisters to see if they could get Mubarak a job at MCI where they were currently working. Shortly thereafter, they said that they could help him. After I talked to Mubarak about my plan he astonishingly agreed to try it one more time. He said that things weren't looking very well in Saudi with the war lingering on. He planned to meet Khalid and me in Maryland where we would get an apartment nearby my sisters.

Dad, Khalid, and I drove to Maryland to meet Mubarak. It was a long trip to say the least. Mom wanted to come along but couldn't get away from her job. My dad was very relaxed and seemed to enjoy the trip, although, he did light up his pipe every two hours when it was inevitably time for Khalid to have a restroom break.

When we arrived my dad stayed to visit for awhile and then flew back home. He and my mom were still in the automobile business and were nice enough to give us the car. Mubarak and my sisters had already found an apartment for us, so we spent the night in our new home. Khalid was very happy and continuously running around exploring the inside and outside. Khalid absolutely loved to walk barefoot on the soft grass, as I did. Khalid seemed mesmerized by all of the lightning bugs sparkling up the night. It was a first for him to see lightning bugs; whereas, the only thing flying around In Saudi Arabia was the sand and now, the black, oily dust.

Mubarak seemed to be very happy and enjoyed his job at first or so I thought. My instinct thought otherwise. After a month I detected that something was wrong with Mubarak's attitude. My oldest sister said that Mubarak couldn't adjust to having a woman as his boss.

One night he said that he decided we should go back to Saudi Arabia. He said that he didn't feel that he belonged in the states. I immediately replied, "Well, now you know how I felt about living in a strange country." He told me that we were going back and that was final. I said, "No I'm not." He said that I had no choice in the matter. I was his wife, and I had to do as he said; otherwise, he would take Khalid away from me, and I would never see him again. He said the cards were in his hands.

I called my sister, Lisa who said that Khalid and I could hide out in her house until Mubarak left. He didn't know where her house was since she had just recently moved. My other sister said that it wouldn't work. He would find us. My only option was to go back to Saudi Arabia. I knew I had to give up my life forever in the United States in order to keep my son. And so I did.

Unwillingly, I went back but was very disturbed about how life could be so cruel. I told myself the time would come when Khalid and I would come back to America. But for now I was going back to what I truly believed was a prison for women; nevertheless, I would continue to suffer for my son. I knew in my heart it would be a long time before I would ever see the beautiful green trees, grass, snow, or lightning bugs again. It would be a long time before I would hear Khalid's giggles as he picked up the lightening bugs. I, of course, was right. It was going to be a long grueling five years before I would ever travel to the United States again.

21. Back to Riyadh

We went back to Riyadh on the Saudi Arabian Airlines. Before we boarded the plane Mubarak told me to put on my abiyah and scarf, but that I could leave the veil off my face until we reached Saudi. I asked him why I had to wear it on the plane. He said because it will be full of Arabs. I was thankful it was a direct flight. Still, fifteen hours is a long time on a plane with a toddler. However, Khalid was a very good and happy world traveler. I was glad to be with my little boy. As the plane was landing though, I started getting that butterfly feeling in my stomach. I didn't want to live here anymore. Furthermore, I didn't want to put the veil over my face. I wanted to be free as well as be able to breathe, because I knew it would be hard to breathe through that black material in the heat of the summer. Black undoubtedly attracted heat. Of course the men wore very thin white robes to stay cool, so they weren't as bothered by the heat as the women.

We exited the plane. As I checked through customs, the security for some reason wouldn't let Khalid or me pass through. Mubarak said they were giving me a hard time because I was an American. I whispered to Mubarak that I had a Bible in my suitcase. He retorted, "Are you crazy?"

The heat in the airport seemed to consistently increase to a very uncomfortable level. I was starting to get dizzy with my face covered from the black veil. Furthermore, I kept thinking about the Bible and a huge blue, handmade decorative glass cross that I had hidden in my suitcase between my clothes. My mom had it made for me so I wanted it to be with me wherever I went. I was thinking that if they find the cross I would be history. They might even shoot me right then and there. I was really starting to feel sick now. Why didn't they have the air conditioner working? How could I be so stupid as to put my life in danger by bringing that Bible and of all things a cross? I told Mubarak that I needed some air, or I was going to pass out. He started arguing with the security guards and told them to let me through. The airport security asked Mubarak why he had married an American. They continued to anger Mubarak to no avail. Mubarak told them one more time that Khalid and I had our entry visas and all our papers and to let us pass. Mubarak said that he had friends in the government, and he was going to call them if they wouldn't let us through. I decided that I would purposely pass out then the security guards would have to pick me up. That might distract them from looking so thoroughly in my suitcase. By this time Khalid was hot and grouchy and started fussing and crying really loudly. Then, just as I was about to fall over on the counter they said tu fudully (go ahead). I was free to go. I passed by security and flipped off my veil so I could finally get some air.

It was amazing how long that took, and I was even married to an Arab. Mubarak told me that was the dumbest thing that I had ever done---putting a Bible and a cross in my suitcase. He said the security and military would have killed me if they found that. He said, "And what do you propose to do with that huge cross?" I responded that I wanted to hang it on a wall. He said, "No way." I told him that I believe in the cross that Jesus died on. He let me know in no uncertain terms that the citizens and Mutaween in Saudi Arabia do not want to have anything to do with Christianity. Mubarak said that they don't understand about what people do in other countries because many of the citizens haven't been anywhere else. It didn't sound like I was going to be able to hang my cross up because if I did I would be killed. My stubbornness wasn't helping matters because if I didn't learn how to live like the Arabs my head might be getting chopped off in the near future.

22. Back to His Parent's House

We had to go back to Mubarak's parent's house to live for a while. Mubarak gave up the apartment we had upon making his decision to move back to the USA. We had to live in that same hot room on the roof again. I'm sure I could have fried an egg on the patio of that roof but never did try it. I was just imagining how Khalid would have loved to just jump on the egg if I had tried frying one there.

About a week after we arrived, Mubarak's mom was having a lot of tea parties. Almost everyday she would ask me to come and join a group of ten to fifteen women. Since my Arabic was better, I could understand what they were saying. Unfortunately, I didn't agree with their philosophy about most subjects. I would also speak up now since I could speak Arabic and tell my opinion which they didn't seem to like. They watched me eat with my left hand and told me that my food was going straight to the devil's stomach. I was not supposed to eat with my left hand. I said that I wrote and ate with my left hand since I was a small child and that was the most ridiculous thing that I ever heard. Mubarak had previously told me to learn to eat with my right hand. He said, "It will make life a lot easier for you." Evidently left handed people in Arabia were outcasts. People there don't use silverware to eat with, so it wasn't that hard to eat with my right hand. It just felt really weird to me, but Mubarak said that it was an insult to their culture if I didn't do things the Arabic way. I was just basically stubborn, and it was the idea of the whole thing. For one thing, I liked to eat with my left hand since

I had been doing it from the time I was a baby, and I had a hard time believing that if I ate with my left hand, food would go to the devil and not my stomach. Finally, I gave in and began using my right hand for everything. Barka, Mubarak's mother, said that food tastes better when you eat with your hands. I thought that was ridiculous, too but decided that it wouldn't help to tell her how I felt about that.

One day when I went to meet Barka's women friends, I blew up at the women because they said that my mom was going straight to hell because she was a Christian. They said that I needed to teach her about Islam and change her to a Muslim. I said that I knew my mom very well, and she will live the rest of her life as a Christian and never change. Then they reminded me again that she was an atheist and was going to hell. I told them that she was not an atheist and was not going to hell. They insisted that all Christians were all going to hell, and I said "You are crazy and you will go to hell then, too." I told Barka that I was sorry to be so outspoken and would like to excuse myself. I abruptly stood up, gave the women a grim stare, walked away, and slammed the door to the room. It was funny how I never did see those women ever again. Maybe they were scared that if they hung out with an American atheist they might go to hell as well. I wasn't sure but presumed they must have been neighbors who were visiting for the afternoon. Barka never did say anything much about that day. She only said, "Some women just like to talk bull and cause problems." Mubarak said that he heard I was pretty angry with some women. I told him that these women said that my mother was going to hell and that I had the right to stand up for my mother. He laughed and said that there are just some uneducated women in Arabia that don't know anything about the world or Christianity. I told him, "That doesn't give them the right to act like God and presume that my mother is atheist and is going to hell when they don't even know her!" I was really upset over the entire situation.

After that incident I was thankful when the Korean Embassy called for me to come back and teach English for them. I knew I would die if I had to sit, drink tea and converse with these grouchy, hard-headed women day after day. I told the principal that I would be there immediately, which was the next day. I was hoping to make enough money to get us living off this roof. Mubarak's mother and sisters gracefully offered to watch Khalid while I went to work. I recall one time when I gave Mubarak's mom some money for food or whatever she needed. I wanted to thank her for letting us live in her home. She literally threw the money right back in my face. Shocked at her actions my thoughts were that I might have done something wrong again that had to do with their custom. I told Mubarak that was rather rude of her. He said that she wouldn't take the money from me. It would have to be given to her from him. Then I watched as he gave her the money. Thankfully, she did take it. I thought that was a bit strange, but a lot of things were strange to me in this country.

23. The Villa

*M*ubarak finally found a job as a manager and finally started back to work. It was only a short time before we moved into a villa nearby his family. I realized that he was going to stay by his parents no matter how hard I pleaded to be closer to the city. His family lived in the outskirts of the desert which was near the Empty Quarter. The Rub' al Khali is the name of the Empty Quarter in Arabic. There is a legend that many people had traveled through this area and never returned. That stretch of desert went on for miles. Mubarak said that anyone traveling through that area would be darn lucky if they met any Bedouins there to help them survive the harsh environment. Most of the Bedouins lived in the outskirts of the Empty Quarter. He also said that the jinns (demons) come out at night in the Empty Quarter, and that's why it is thought that so many people don't return alive. That was interesting and a bit hard to believe. I really didn't feel like checking it out alone though. I would definitely need a camel and as grouchy as they are I don't know if I would be able to go a long distance with one on such a trip. Mubarak made it sound like it was the Bermuda Triangle or worse. I discovered that the Empty Quarter is one of the largest sand deserts in the world and is about the size of Texas. The Empty Quarter does indeed have many mysterious secrets. One of the largest oil fields in the world exists in this area. Millions of years ago this area was a tropical rainforest where water buffalo roamed as well as hippos. There is said to be a lost city or even an entire lost civilization here called the Iram of the Pillars. There have been a few artifacts found in this so called lost city. There were many tribes that existed in this area. Mubarak said one tribe had helped him and his friends when their jeep broke down in the middle of nowhere. He said they would have died whereas the temperatures reach to 131 degrees Fahrenheit. He also had been bitten by a scorpion, and the people of the tribes knew what to do to prevent the poison from killing him.

The villa where we moved was old and had huge bugs crawling around that Khalid liked to chase and kill. I vividly remember seeing a beehive on our balcony that was about four feet long. I grabbed Khalid, who was exploring, on his way out there. Thank goodness I had seen it before he grabbed it. I told Mubarak, and he eventually had somebody take it away. That was another strange incidence. I had never seen such a large beehive so close to a house. In fact, as long as I had been living in Saudi I hadn't seen one bee. What a shock! As soon as we settled in the house I told Mubarak that I was pregnant again. Obviously, he was happy about that since he was planning to have a huge family.

For the first time since I had been in Riyadh, I made a really good friend with the woman who lived in the villa below us. She was about the same age as I. She spoke Arabic slowly so I could understand her. Her name was Zahada. We would visit each other on a regular basis and take each other food. She taught me how to make different kinds of Arabic dishes. She had a little girl and boy whom Khalid loved to play with. Zahada treated Khalid as one of her own and was very caring as well. Some nights she would send us supper as she knew I was pregnant and working. She told me to stay home and not go to work, but I told her that I loved helping the Korean children learn English. I would also sit with her children and help them study English when I had some free time.

I went to check on Zahada one day since I hadn't seen her in two weeks. As she opened the door I saw her limping. She said that she couldn't see through her black veil and had tripped as she was going down the steps and as a result she broke her leg. After that incident she told her husband that she wanted to wear the veil that had holes cut out for the eyes so that she could see where she was going. Her husband said that he would think about it. I told her to just do it unless she wanted to break her other leg, too. Many women wore these types of veils- including me. Unfortunately, Mubarak didn't like the men staring at my green eyes. He recently had made me cover my eyes when we went to the farmer's market or to a shop. I noticed it was especially difficult for the women who lived out of the city limits not to cover their eyes. The people were more backward, unlike the people living in the city. This was one of the reasons that I kept asking Mubarak to let us move to the city. There were also huge shopping malls, bookstores, and restaurants there. All the women who walked around in the city had to wear their Abiyahs of course, but there was a little more freedom in the city.

Riyadh even had a Burger King and was in the process of building a McDonalds, although I heard that they didn't use hamburger for the meat. Somebody told me it was ground-up lamb.

Whereas, the area where we lived had very small shops and restaurants that only served chicken and rice or schwarmas, which is meat wrapped in pita bread. Women are also forbidden to go in the restaurants in this area.

Women are allowed in the restaurants in the city, but only in the women allowed door or area. I did not like the idea of being desegregated which made it seem that women were far less superior to men. This was their law of course and what the Saudi's believed was right. Strange men were to stay away from the women and children for their safety or so it is said.

Me and Khalid; cushions on floor used as couches

24. The Vacation

*M*ubarak must have felt sorry for me not being able to see my family and travel anywhere, so he said that he would take Khalid and me to the United Arab Emirates for a short vacation. Since his brother, Solomon, lived there, we had a free tour guide. I was about four months pregnant at the time and wasn't showing much, so I was able to wear a swimsuit that Mubarak bought me to wear to the beach. There was a lot more freedom in the Emirates. I just had to cover my head with a scarf but still wore the abiyah in the city. At the hotel the women were wearing bikinis, so I put mine on, too. I couldn't believe that Mubarak was allowing me to wear a bikini. He didn't seem concerned at all since there were many British and American tourists staying in the hotel. They were all wearing modern attire. The pool was amazing. It had a huge waterfall with a slide next to it that Khalid couldn't seem to get enough of. There was also a bar in the pool and a bar on the beach. The sand was white as snow. There was also a little putt-putt golf course where Khalid loved to play. Everything, including the putt- putt, was nearby the pool. Khalid was having a great time, and we could keep our eyes on him as he wandered from place to place. It was all very nice except Mubarak, for some reason, refused to buy suntan lotion for Khalid or me. He said that we didn't need it because he never used it. As a result Khalid and I both ended up having horrible sunburns. Well, me more than Khalid. Since I was blonde with a light complexion, I became as red as a beet. I told Mubarak that I was working, and I needed some of my money to buy lotion. My pleading didn't work, so I told him that I wasn't going to give him anymore of the money that I made if he refused. He said that he only had Saudi dollars and that I would have to change it somewhere. So I did at the front desk in the hotel. I got the notion that he thought it was quite funny that I had a sunburn, but Khalid didn't deserve that treatment. I did buy suntan lotion, goggles, and other items that we needed. Of course Mubarak then decided that he needed suntan lotion since he was now getting burned. Such nerve that man had. I told him to buy his own because Khalid and I were going to use the entire bottle. I learned from that mistake but knew that he would get me back for not giving him any of my lotion. I was too angry and burned at the time to deal with his little mind games.

That day I decided that I would only give Mubarak enough money to buy food for the house. I would save the rest and when I had the chance to get back home, I would put it in a bank in the United States. I wondered why somebody always had to take me to the limit before I got my independence back somehow.

That afternoon on the beach we met a young boy that didn't speak any English. He reminded me of Mowgli from the Jungle Book for some reason. He climbed to the top of a coconut tree and pulled a coconut off the tree and brought it down to me and Khalid. The boy cracked it open and gave us some juice along with the coconut. Khalid ate it even though it tasted bitter. That was the first time I had ever had a coconut straight out of a tree. Khalid tried to climb the tree after the boy— to no avail of course.

One night in Abu Dhabi we went to see a belly dancer while Mubarak's brother watched Khalid. She was wearing a green, silky, sparkling traditional garb. She had those little cymbals strapped on her fingers and snapped them continuously as she danced and twirled around. She was of course very entertaining and made it look so easy. It also looked like she was getting some high dollars from the Arab sheiks. She danced similar to my Egyptian girlfriends.

Later on we went to a night club that was full of American soldiers. I knew that Mubarak wouldn't like it there because of the Americans and sure enough, he started a fight with somebody who was talking to me. That ended that evening out, so we drove back to the hotel. Except for getting sunburned, it was a week of relaxation away from the stringent rules of Arabia.

25. Nadia

I was finally getting into the last stages of my pregnancy. Mubarak was making me take long walks in order to make my delivery much easier, so he said. His mom actually told him to keep me walking. She said it would help me. One day he took me to the town square where there were a lot of people walking through shops. At the end of the street I noticed a huge block of stone. This is where murderers are beheaded. The court also assigns someone to behead those who renounce Islam. They also cut off the right hand of a person who steals. Furthermore, this is where women are stoned to death for committing adultery. I was stunned that they still resort to such barbaric methods. Mubarak also informed me that a huge crowd of men come weekly to watch. I asked if women were allowed to watch. He said no. It was considered too harsh for a woman to watch such tactics. Nonetheless, I wouldn't want to watch such a dreadful sight, especially the stoning of a woman. I was suddenly tired of walking and thinking about this place. I then asked Mubarak to take us home.

I was having pains in my stomach all morning and knew that it was time for the baby to come. Mubarak took me to the doctor who told me to go back home because it would be a couple of hours before it was time. By midnight that night it was time. I yelled for Mubarak, but he wouldn't get up. He said that it wasn't time yet. I could not believe that he went back to sleep. I began wondering if I would be able to deliver it alone since he wouldn't take me to the hospital. I went into the bathroom to throw some cold water on my face when some water gushed out of me onto the floor. Then I felt horrible pain and the baby moving downward. I thought this is it. I can not do this alone in the bathroom. I went to the bedroom and pushed Mubarak out of bed, and I told him that I was not going to have the baby alone in the house. I told him my water broke and to move it. He got up then, and we went to the car.

This baby didn't want to wait for time or anybody. I barely made it to the hospital, and there she was. It was a girl. She had to have an Arabic name so I chose Nadia because I remembered my flight attendant friend who was always there when I needed somebody to talk to. I remembered telling her that if I ever had a little girl, I would name her Nadia. Nadia had dark brown hair and eyes like Khalid. She was a beautiful baby. As she grew to the toddler stage, she began resembling my mom and my Gram Schiller. Both have dark brown eyes, dark brown hair, and mom has a dark complexion as well.

26. All Alone

When Nadia was about two years old Mubarak said that he was going to take a trip to the Empty Quarter. I said, "Why do you want to go where you said the jinns are?" He said that there was a sheik with a lot of power that would sign a paper for him to get the Saudi Citizenship. (He was a Yemeni citizen by origin.) Then he could get a better job and not have to worry about getting a visa to stay in Saudi. He said that they would have to cross the desert on camel because there weren't any roads. I asked him if I could go. He said that I was crazy. A woman would die out there or the jinns (demons) would get you. They were taking ten men along and would have to sleep on the ground at night. He said that he would be back in about two weeks. He told his brothers to check on us everyday to see if we needed anything. As soon as Mubarak left, Khalid started a fever. It was 103 degrees so I called Ahmad and Abdullah to please take Khalid to the hospital. They arrived in five minutes and took us to the doctor who determined that Khalid had the measles. Mubarak's brothers bought us some food and medicine that the doctor prescribed. I couldn't believe how good they were to me after Mubarak left. They were on the ball, unlike Mubarak who didn't even stock the house with anything before his journey to the desert. I wondered at times how he could be so forgetful with two children and a wife to take care of. Furthermore, why were so many people in the family asking if Mubarak was in his right mind or not? I needed to get to the bottom of this.

One night Mubarak's uncle Omar came to visit with his wife Hayah. I had never met a woman with a name like that. She was very nice though even though her husband was the uncle who made trouble for Mubarak in Houston. I tried to be hospitable, but only because I liked his wife and children. She told me that she was pregnant with twins and seemed very happy. Then she asked me how Mubarak's mind was. She said that he was not right in his head. I told her that I never gave it much thought. I told her that I think we're all a bit strange. I think I'm strange for living in Arabia. On the other hand, I often wondered why he seemed to forget things that he did after only a short time. I blamed it on the homemade moonshine that he had recently been drinking. Mubarak showed me how highly toxic it was by pouring some in a spoon. After it was lit the flames turned purple as they rose in the air. It smelled like rubbing alcohol. I told him to keep that stuff far away from me. In our religion we believed that our body was a temple of God, so that liquid wasn't going into my temple. In Islam alcohol was forbidden. In my opinion he wasn't being a very devout Muslim, but nobody is perfect in this life.

We all have our little qualms or bad habits. I think he was going a bit too far with this homemade alcohol, but it was his stomach of course, not mine.

This made me think about what my grandma always told me. We can eat and do anything in life, but we must always do it in moderation. She said that's what God has tried to teach us; otherwise, we will be sorry. I think she was right in her saying as she was one hundred years old July 14, 2009, and she does everything in moderation.

Omar said that Mubarak wasn't in his right mind to let us live in such an old villa and leave us alone like he had. He added that when Mubarak was little, he was caught drinking gasoline. After that his mind was never the same again. That was the strangest thing I had ever heard. Well, I take that back because the longer I was living among the Arabs the stranger the stories were getting. I told them that however his mind may be that I was his wife, and I was the one who had to put up with it. They both visited awhile longer while the children played.

That next week I heard that Hayah, her maid, and her children were killed in a fire. Omar was away on business in Dammam. When he came home he saw his wife and children wrapped in white sheets laying out in a row on the porch.

He was devastated for quite some time after that. So was I for that matter. Her family said that she was found lying next to the door. It was the door leading to the roof, and the neighbors nearby had locked the door from the outside keeping her from getting out. What a horrible way to die. I was wondering why the neighbors locked the door to the roof, but I heard from the family that the roof was part of the house next door which belonged to the neighbors so they had the right to keep the door locked. If only they would have left it open that night Heya and her children would have survived. Is it fate or was it written?

That night I was wondering if Mubarak had been killed. Why would he want to go through the Empty Quarter when so many people didn't make it across that desert? He must have wanted those papers signed very badly. Now I realized how it must be for him being a Yemeni living in Saudi Arabia. Another week passed, and I didn't hear a word about him. I wondered how I would know if he made it or not. There wasn't anyway that he could make contact with me. I just waited although it was scary at times, especially at night being an American all alone in a foreign country. I was lucky that his brothers came to check on us.

Khalid was doing better with his measles but still had spots all over his body. It was wintertime, and the rooms become very cold-especially at night.

One night I heard someone walking around on the patio in the villa. I knew that my neighbor Zahada was gone visiting her family for awhile. Then I heard a loud click and our electricity went out and naturally, our big heater for the house went out. At first I was worried if the man that I saw through the window was a thief. I got up to double check that the door to our villa was locked, and it was. I kept Khalid and Nadia close to me in the bedroom until I heard a door slam in the patio downstairs. I opened the window to look out, and I saw a man leaving. There had to be a reason that somebody turned our electricity off. I checked the telephones to call Mubarak's brothers and the line was dead. Now what? I would have to wait until the morning and walk to his mom and dad's house with the children and stay there until

Mubarak came back. I didn't think that he would be gone so long. It had been three weeks. I had been so busy with work at school and then Khalid and Nadia took up my time when I had gotten home that the days just went by.

Nadia kept shaking and saying it is cold. I got out our small heater that thankfully was battery operated and took it to the bedroom. We all ended up sleeping together to keep warm which was very cozy. Sometimes I found it hard to believe that I was living in the middle of the desert, and we were all freezing to death.

The next morning I heard somebody walking upstairs. It was him. He made it back. He said that he got his papers signed. He showed me where he was bitten by a scorpion. There was a huge black and green mark on his foot. It was bruised about the size of a baseball. He said that he was sick for awhile but obviously, pulled through. They said he would have died if the poison wasn't removed immediately. Luckily, a Bedouin man had drained out the poison. Even though many people die from the most poisonous bites the Bedouins are used to being bitten by scorpions and generally survive.

He said they had to ride camels most of the time. Mubarak said that it was terribly uncomfortable and never wanted to do that again. They had a truck with them at first to help take supplies, but naturally it broke down. They met some Bedouins who helped them find their way to the Sheik. He said it was unbelievable how the Sheik had his own little city in the middle of the desert. It sounded like a movie, and I wish I could have gone along until I heard about the scorpions.

27. Mecca

After Mubarak received the Saudi Citizenship he found a better job. Then we moved into a huge, beautiful villa. It had three bathrooms, a huge kitchen, and six other large rooms. There was also a huge room outside on the patio where the men would sit together and smoke their sheesha and drink. Sheesha was a type of tobacco that was put into a huge bong that the men smoked all the time. It had a long hose connected to a mouthpiece on the end for breathing in the smoke. I had tried it once to see what the men were smoking and found it to be very strong. Mubarak said that they filled it with fruit tobacco, but I often wondered about that. It was stronger than taking a puff out of my dad's old pipe. I used to do that when I was younger when he wasn't looking. It was awful, and I started coughing and then dad said, "What did you just do? "Oh nothing," I mumbled. He replied, "I know what you did."

After we moved into the new villa, I realized we didn't have a phone. Mubarak said there were no phone connections out this far from the city; however, he had bought a cell phone. I knew then that this time we were very far from the city. The roads weren't even paved. There was only a small sandy dirt path through the desert to get to our villa. The reason I agreed to move so quickly was because my neighbor Zahada moved into the same building in the villa below us, but I had no idea that we would be living this far out. There were a few houses around but no shops. I noticed a lot of sheep crossing the dirt road, so I presumed we were close to a farm. Mubarak urged me to stop working since he was making such good money now. I agreed to stay home with Khalid and Nadia who were my only solace during these lonely and hard times.

My Arabic continued to improve as I spent my days visiting Zahada. Mubarak was helping me as well. He was also pushing the Islamic religion on me more and more. He said that he was planning to take me to Mecca to learn more about Islam.

The following month Mubarak drove us to Jeddah, and we would continue our journey to Mecca the following day. The Red Sea was awesome! I tried to imagine what it would look as the waters spread apart as it was told in the Bible. Because it was so clear, I had overheard the British and Americans loved to go scuba diving in this sea.

I noticed that most of the women didn't cover their faces in Jeddah, so I didn't either. Many of them only covered their heads with the black scarves.

We stayed at a hotel that resembled a castle. When we went out to eat Khalid and Nadia thought they were so cool drinking orange juice out of fancy champagne glasses. I often wondered how Mubarak could afford such an extravagant hotel. He hadn't been working at his new job for that long.

The next morning we left for Mecca. When we arrived at the border there was a checkpoint with ten military men. As the men approached the car, Mubarak abruptly told me to cover my face. Fortunately, there weren't any problems. He told me that I was very lucky because Americans weren't allowed in Mecca. He said that I had to recite some verses from the Qur'an if I were asked to do so. I knew enough of it by now to get through. On our way to Mecca all there was to see was the dusty brown desert and a few wild camels. I still missed trees and cows.

When we arrived I was astonished at how huge the mosque was. Since we were making umrah (to ask forgiveness from all sins which was required before making Hajj), we had to cover ourselves with white cloth which was much better to wear than black in the heat of the day. The temperature was at least a hundred and thirty degrees. As far as I could see the floor was made of marble. Impulsively, I took off my sandals to feel the soft, cool marble on my feet. The marble covered more than an area of a huge shopping mall parking lot. We had to walk on the marble for about ten minutes until we finally reached the mosque. Mubarak led me through the mosque which again had marble floors with huge pillars of marble surrounding the building. He said that we had to walk around in circles about a hundred times and pray for forgiveness of our sins as we walked. In Arabic one would say ushtugful Allah which in English is forgive me my sins. As a person walked they would continuously say this phrase. After awhile Mubarak put Khalid on his shoulders, and I pushed Nadia in her stroller. This seemed strange to just keep walking around in circles. We must have walked for miles because the mosque was huge. Then Mubarak showed me a spring where water was shooting straight up from the ground. Mubarak said the first wife of Abraham pleaded with God to give her and her children water after they were stranded in the desert. Ishmael was one of the children. Abraham had gone to the mountains to pray, at this time and hadn't returned. The Muslims say that this was the spring that God made for her and her children, and thus they survived the harsh conditions of the desert. This became the site for the holy mosque in Mecca. There was the most beautiful marble that I have ever seen which was built around the spring as water gushed upward from the ground. I didn't remember this story from the Bible. I loved to learn about history, and this was very interesting. Next, we went to walk around the Kaba. This was the most famous place in the world for Muslims. Only Muslims were allowed to walk around the Kaba. Christians were not allowed. Mubarak first showed me a footprint that was said to be Abraham's. His footprint was embedded on a marble pedestal surrounded by glass. The footprint was huge. It was approximately fifteen inches long and very wide. Abraham's footprint was saved because he and his son, Ishmael, built the Kaba which was to be a place for all Muslims to pray. Mubarak motioned for me to move toward the Kaba. He said that the people won't stop walking in circles. I should stay alert so as not to get knocked over. The women had their black abiyahs (capes) on as they were walking around the Kaba. They were just praying though, not making Umrah. The people were moving quickly and pushing aggressively. I carried Nadia so she wouldn't get trampled, and he carried Khalid. Suddenly Mubarak grabbed my arm and said to move closer to the Kaba. I held Nadia tighter because the closer I moved toward the Kaba the more aggressive the crowd became. I noticed the Kaba was covered with a suede black material, and the name Allah was written and was embellished with gold as well as other intricate designs. Mubarak grabbed my arm again and pulled me closer toward a hole in the Kaba. He said that I should put my head in this hole. I told him no. As I got closer to the black hole people were pushing violently trying to put their heads inside. They were literally knocking each other over to get in there. There is a legend that says this is the only place in the world where you could smell the heavens. Mubarak took Nadia and told me to go and push my way in. So I did. It was dark in there and cold. Then I smelled something like incense. I thought, "Well, we had incense on earth so what was the big deal?" It didn't convince me that this was what heaven smelled like. I don't think we are supposed to know that anyway. Why did heaven have only one smell? Heaven might have a million scents or none at all for all we know. Suddenly a woman knocked me out of the hole. I decided to keep my thoughts to myself and let Mubarak go and give it a try. He said that it smelled like perfume to him. Then we continued walking in circles around the Kaba. The people were going amazingly fast. I was starting to get tired having to continuously hold Nadia for fear she would get lost and trampled on. She was also getting fussy.

I told Mubarak that we were going to find somewhere to sit down. I found it strange that I didn't have to cover my face here. Nobody seemed to care either. Why was it so forbidden in Riyadh and not other places in the kingdom especially the most religious place in the kingdom? I had too many questions with too few answers.

It made me think about Christianity even more, and how I missed it. At times some of the people seemed so barbaric in Saudi. They rarely said thank you or I'm sorry. They didn't seem to know what it meant to stand in line and wait for something. They just knocked each other out of the way as they had at the hole in the Kaba. They did this at shops and markets as well. I was getting tired of thinking. I sat down on the smooth marble floor and held Nadia. I was ever so grateful just to have her by my side. Khalid came running over to me and said that he was getting tired of walking. Mubarak followed shortly thereafter. We decided to leave and went to get something to eat. We ate some schwarma's (grilled chicken wrapped in pita bread with horseradish mixed with mayonnaise) and looked through some shops. Mubarak told me that I was very lucky to see the holy site of Mecca. Americans are forbidden to enter, but I was considered a Muslim as I knew how to pray and had memorized many verses of the Quran by now. Mubarak told me that I was a Muslim, but I knew in my heart that I was always Christian and always would be. He said that I could be killed if I said that I was a Christian. That gave me the chills but then anger set in. I was tired of being threatened because of my nationality and religion. Still, I continued to teach the Bible to Khalid when Mubarak was gone. I hid the Bible and my cross in the closet. I also had a children's Bible that I kept hidden as well. I could have been killed if anyone had found those, but my faith was strong helping me to not feel afraid while I was living in the Middle East.

Since then I have had encounters with many people who think the Muslims have a different God then the Christians, but each pray to the same God just as the Jews do even though there are a few major differences in each religion. The Muslims believe that Jesus was taken up in the sky to his father but not crucified. They believe that God put another man on the cross who looked like Jesus; therefore, Jesus wouldn't have to suffer such bodily pain. Mubarak said that God wouldn't want to hurt his only son. Muslims also believe that Mary was not the mother of God and that the Christians would be punished at the end of the world for believing in such blasphemy. The Muslims also said that the Christians were wrong about the Sabbath that God needed to rest on the seventh day. Mubarak said they believed that God didn't need to rest. God was all powerful and never got tired. I realized that I could argue all day with Mubarak and any Muslim on these issues but felt that it would be more wise to keep silent at given times. It was too dangerous to disagree with all the radical Muslims everywhere. The Taliban and Mutaween were, and still are, too extreme for me, so I kept quiet for the safety of my children. I also have respect for all religions and nationalities. Everyone should have the right to their own beliefs.

28. Moving and Teaching Again

*M*ubarak found yet another new job and decided to move again. We kept moving further and further away from the city. There were only sandy dirt roads to drive on to get to the house. This time we lived on the bottom of a villa and another family, who owned the villa, lived above us. As I walked in the door I noticed that the floors were covered in a smooth grayish- marble. The bathrooms had marble floors and walls as well. Saudi Arabia is blessed with an abundance of marble and oil, that is for sure. Mubarak said he only paid ten American cents to fill his gas tank. It was unbelievable! The villa had three huge living rooms, a dining area, three bedrooms, a spacious kitchen, three bathrooms and a huge porch. The rooms were very large. My guess was that since most Arabs had between seven and twelve children, there had to be big houses built to live comfortably with such big families. There was a door in the dining room that led to the villa upstairs. The neighbors kept it locked. This is how I would visit my new neighbor. Her name was Fatima. She invited me to visit the first night in our house. She was a heavyset girl with large brown eyes and short dark brown hair. She had a very bubbly personality. I noticed that she would wear sleeveless shirts and tight pants at times. She would wear jeans, too. I was thankful that she wasn't one of those religious extremists. From what I observed she was far from it but was devoted to her religion just the same. She had more of an open mind. She liked to get out of the house and take walks which was a treat for me to finally have somebody to escape the confines of the home. She didn't cover her eyes because she said that she couldn't see where she was going and had tripped a few times herself especially when wearing high heels.

Boredom was getting the best of me again. I decided to look for another English teaching job. I was in luck! There was one opening at the Diplomatic Quarters to teach English to the Princes' children. I was hired by the principal and accepted the position. I was going to be paid more than Mubarak could have ever dreamed at the time. However, I was a bit leery at first since I knew these children came from such wealthy families. I noticed they seemed a bit spoiled, but their positive attitude and eagerness to study English and learn about the American culture outweighed the other negativity. They implored me to teach them how to play basketball and baseball. I was surprised when the principal told me to take them outside to teach them how to play some American sports. So I did. They loved to play softball and basketball and caught on to the game quickly. I couldn't believe that I was getting paid to teach them how to play games, but it was a good experience for them to learn as much as they could about another culture. I stayed for a couple of months at the Diplomatic Quarters until I was offered a third grade teaching position at a private British school that was also called the Liberian Embassy School, although there was only one child from Liberia. The school used the British system of teaching and there were a few teachers from London who taught there. The other teachers were from Australia, Lebanon, Canada, India, and two from America.

Khalid was attending this school, and I had been waiting to work at the same school. I was lucky again for such a position to open up as one of the British teachers' decided to retire and go back to London. The principal was from New Mexico in the United States. It was an excellent school! The students even had swimming lessons once a week at an indoor pool at the school. I soon found out that my students were of many different nationalities. They were from Lebanon, Britain, Germany, Saudi, India, Canada, Greece, Australia and one from France.

My one student from France had a hard time keeping up as her English was not very good, but she eventually did catch up with the rest of the students. I finally had found something in my life that I really enjoyed doing that didn't seem like work. I loved the children like my own. After my first 18 months of teaching, I found out that I was pregnant again. I was fortunate not to have morning sickness this time. I decided to keep teaching until the time of my delivery.

Unfortunately, one day some mutowahs (Taliban) came to our school. I saw them out of my window and put my book down on my desk. The students must have known something was wrong by my actions. My room was on the second floor of the building. We had a pretty good view of what was going on in the front of the building. Of course the boys stood up and looked out the window and shouted mutowahs (religious extremists). The girls looked worried. I told the boys to get back from the windows and sit down. Suddenly there was a knock at the door. It was the secretary who told me to keep all the students in the room and lock the door. There were some men coming. I knew who they were and locked the door. I prayed that they wouldn't come bother us especially being seven months pregnant. This wasn't a good time for fighting with any men or to be taken away by them. I had heard some terrible stories of what they did to American women or other women for that matter. I kept my faith in the principal that she would be able to take care of the problem.

I told the students that we would do some silent reading for awhile. The students knew it was time to be quiet and read their books. I gazed through the window as the mutaween walked around the playground. I knew that I should be reading my book so the students wouldn't think that anything was wrong, but it had been an hour. They still weren't leaving. I was getting worried about the principal who was from America. I knew the mutaween didn't like Americans. The mutaween thought that Americans were atheist and refused to believe otherwise. Finally, I saw them leave and was grateful they didn't come to our room. We had a meeting after school, and the principal said that the mutaween (religious extremists) were going to close the school down. They would allow us to finish the year out, but it was not to be reopened. From now on all schools had to be licensed under the Saudi government, and they had to teach the Quran. I didn't know that this school was kept undercover until now. As I mentioned before we were teaching the British curriculum, and it was called the Liberian Embassy School. However, there weren't any students from Liberia that attended except one. Living in Riyadh I knew that it was difficult for parents to find good schools for their children to attend. I wondered where all of these children would go. Many of the parents said they were going back to their countries because it was too hard on their children to live this way. The parents wanted their freedom back and wanted the same for their children. The mutaween were starting to have more control over the city everyday.

Khalid, of course, had to tell Mubarak about the mutaween coming to school. Mubarak said that since I was an American it might be getting too dangerous for me to be out teaching if the mutaween were out checking on the schools. He said that after the baby was born that I was to stay at home again and no more teaching. Mubarak's brother found out as well and said that I had no business working while I was pregnant. I should stay home. So much for having some freedom and to be doing what I loved- teaching children.

29. Sarah

*I*t was a hot September morning when I started feeling the pain. I knew I was going to have to have a caesarean because the doctor said the baby was breech, but I wasn't scheduled to go in for another week. He thought that maybe she would turn around in a week, but evidently she didn't want to wait. I was getting worried that I didn't have anyone to help at home with the children or the house. I told Mubarak in the morning before he went to work, so he said we would go. Naturally, he had to stop by his office first. He ended up making a couple of stops, and when we got to his office the contractions were getting stronger. I told him that the baby was breech, and we should get going to the hospital. He told me he would get me there but then made me sit in the car while he went into his office for about thirty minutes. I wondered who would make a woman who was in labor sit in a hundred and twenty degree temperature for that long. I was getting worried for the baby since I just knew that she wasn't turning around. I didn't even feel her moving at all. Mubarak finally came back, and I told him that the contractions were even closer. Why was he doing this because it was dangerous for the baby as well as me to deliver breech? He said to quit worrying because my contractions were so far apart. I said that they were only eight minutes apart now.

When we finally arrived at the hospital the doctor said that they needed to hurry and get me in the operating room because my contractions were getting closer. The baby was still breech. He said that I could try and deliver normally, but it could be dangerous. He said that he might have to pull her leg to get her out. This could cause her to be damaged for life. He said that it was a high probability that I would suffer, too and be in danger as well. I told him to go ahead with the caesarean. This situation made me really dislike Mubarak because he put both the baby and me in danger. By now I was having horrible contractions of five minutes apart, and two or three nurses were rushing to prep me for surgery. I remember being in the room alone when a nurse came in, told me her name, then suddenly, put her arm up above her head and came down with all her force and stabbed me in the back of my hand with a needle. She then pulled it out and as she did, blood came gushing out. She turned around while another nurse came in the room, yelled at her, and told her to leave the room. Simultaneously, my doctor came in and he too, started yelling in Arabic at the nurse who stabbed me. I remember him telling her to get out and practically chased her out of the room. Then I thought, "Oh great. Is somebody trying to kill me because I'm American? How could this be happening while I am going to have a baby?" My doctor ordered the other nurse to put the needle in my other arm. He said that he was sorry about that incident and security escorted her out of the building. He assured me and exclaimed, "I'm here now and nobody will hurt you!" His nurse took my other arm and said that I would be okay. She gently inserted the needle, and I went to sleep. I often wondered what the deal was with that first nurse. Maybe she really was trying to get rid of me. I was so delirious with pain by that time that I really did not know what was going on. There was definitely something going on. I would ask about it when I got better. As soon as I saw my doctor I was ready to go to sleep. I knew Dr. Abraham for about seven years now and trusted him with my life. He delivered my other two children and was always very good and conscientious about my health. When I woke up the doctor said that I had a girl and her foot was really stuck, so it was a good thing that I agreed to a caesarean. He said that the baby and I were fine. Tests showed that I was anemic, so the doctor decided to keep me in the hospital for a week to recover. I just remember lying in the hospital bed only able to drink liquids, and I was barely able to nurse Sarah who looked healthy and beautiful. I did ask somebody about the name of that nurse who stabbed me. Nobody had heard of that name in the hospital. I asked Mubarak about it. He did hear that something was going on and was getting worried. He said that he saw security chasing a nurse down the hall and things looked pretty chaotic there for awhile. He remarked that it was taken care of and everything is okay. It really had me concerned that nobody knew who that nurse was and why was security chasing her? It was hard for me to sleep at night to say the least. My doctor had someone watch my room which made me feel a little less anxious. Mubarak visited for about fifteen minutes and left. He didn't come back that night or the next morning. He finally stopped by the next night to visit for about thirty minutes and then left. I often wondered about that. I thought that he was probably busy with work. My doctor would check on me at night when he was finished with his rounds. We would sit and talk. He was very intelligent and charming. He asked why Mubarak didn't come to see me. He said that if I were his wife he would be here all the time. I was almost wishing that he was my husband as cold hearted as mine had been lately.

Mubarak stopped by the hospital after the third day and said he was going to bring a maid from Thailand to help take care of the house. He nonchalantly looked at the baby and said that he had to get back to work and walked out the door. For some reason he acted as though he didn't want anything to do with the new baby. He would not pick her up as he did with Khalid and Nadia.

After a week my doctor said that I could go home. We named the baby Sarah. She was a good baby and usually slept through the night-unlike Nadia. Nadia was like a whirlwind. She never needed much sleep and was as stubborn as could be. Nadia reminded me of my mom. I already could tell that Sarah was going to be more docile.

30. The Change

After Sarah and I came home I noticed that Mubarak was drinking more and more moonshine or white lightning as my American husband told me. He said that's most likely what it was that Mubarak was drinking since real alcohol was forbidden and not even sold there. He came home in the afternoon and would start drinking and smoke his sheisha from that big glass pipe. He was becoming more violent as well. One day when we were eating lunch Nadia refused to sit down and eat. Suddenly he pulled the tablecloth out and all the dishes flew up in the air. It was like the movie Titanic when the rich fiance' of Rose knocked all the dishes off the table. All of our new dishes were broken and some pieces flew into Nadia's face and on her body. She was bleeding on her leg and face. I was holding the baby and grabbed Nadia to see how bad the cut was.

Just then, our maid came running to see what was wrong. She helped me clean up the broken dishes and food while the baby was crying, and Nadia was screaming bloody murder. Poor Khalid went to his room to hide for fear of being hit. Mubarak just walked out the door while the maid gave him a dirty look and yelled at him in her own language. She was very shy and didn't speak any English, but she did understand some Arabic. She also didn't seem to be a bit afraid of Mubarak and quickly ran over to pick up the broken dishes. I was surprised to see her running to help me and not be afraid of him.

Mubarak was on a roll with his anger and flighty moods. Some nights he would come home at four in the morning from drinking. He told me to get up out of bed so he could talk to me. I was glad he never came into the bedroom to do his little confrontations because the baby was sleeping in her crib in our room. I quietly shut the bedroom door so as not to awaken the baby and walked into the living room where he was standing. He viciously knocked me over with one arm. I flew back and fell on the floor. Then he started hitting some of the electric outlets in the house with a metal pole. I do not know why he was hitting the electric outlets. At the time I thought what an idiot, and I wondered if he could possibly get electrocuted by doing that. Almost immediately, Khalid came out of the bedroom, and I told him to get back into his room quickly. I knew that Mubarak would take the metal pole and beat Khalid with it. I was trying to figure out where he had got that metal from, but right now my thoughts were on Khalid. Khalid just stood there, and I got up off the floor and told him again to go into his room. Finally, he did while Mubarak went to another room banging on the electrical outlets. It was very weird, and by this time I was almost hoping for him to get shocked or pass out. Fortunately, it was the latter. He passed out in the back room.

I was just glad that he didn't go after Khalid with the metal pole because the week before he had done just that. I was making dinner in the kitchen when Khalid was doing his homework. He was reading the Qur'an. Evidently it wasn't good enough for Mubarak. In addition, his grades in his Arabic studies weren't as high as Mubarak wanted. His English grades were very good, but Mubarak didn't seem to care about that.

Mubarak was upset about his reading the Qur'an so badly and started calling Khalid a donkey and an animal in Arabic. Then he told him that he was very stupid. I came in the room and told him to quit telling the child that he was stupid. He was doing the best that he could with his studies. Mubarak told me to stay out of it. Then he went and got a long metal pole and started hitting Khalid with it. He then grabbed Khalid and put him in his room on the bed and started beating his feet with the metal pole. I jumped in front of Khalid because I told Mubarak that he was going to break his legs. I got whacked a couple of times and grabbed the pole away from him. I told Mubarak to get out of the room, and I said that I was going to take Khalid away if he didn't stop with the verbal and physical abuse. To my surprise he left. I took a deep breath and decided that my planning to leave this country just took a leap forward. Nobody was going to abuse my child like this. Khalid never really cried much. He just said that he thought he really was stupid and that everything was his fault. I told him there was nothing wrong with him that it was his father, not him. I told him that I would figure a way to get us out of here to go back to America to live, but we couldn't let his father know that we weren't ever going to come back to Saudi Arabia.

31. The Maid

At the same time I was dealing with Mubarak's outrages, the maid was another concern. She kept telling me in Arabic that Mubarak promised to send her home. I said that he didn't tell me anything about her leaving.

She did keep the house very clean, but I noticed that she wasn't very friendly with the children. She also didn't want to cook. My neighbor said from her experience with maids was that the maid didn't want me to know that she could cook. One day she was cleaning the leaves of my plants with olive oil. I asked her why she was using oil. She said it makes them shine and nourishes them. She told me that she learned this when she worked for a prince and cleaned his castle. I thought that was cool that I had a maid who had worked for a prince. I asked her what it was like there. She said that the prince had many wives and children. She said that the wives and children ate together. Each wife had her own maid. She said that the wives got along very well together. Mubarak didn't tell me that she had worked for one of the princes. I asked him, and he said yes that was where he had bought her because this prince evidently had plenty of maids and was willing to give one up. She said that she wasn't very happy there, but she didn't seem very happy with us either. She kept telling Mubarak that she wanted to go home. She had been here for many years and wanted to go back to Thailand to see her family. He told her no. She evidently decided to take her frustrations out on us because she was becoming less and less friendly. One morning she was chasing Khalid around the house threatening to hit him with a stick. She also wasn't cleaning very well anymore. Khalid didn't like her and said that we need to get rid of her. I told him that we would have to keep her for awhile because she didn't have anywhere else to go. Mubarak had to apply for her exit visa so she could leave. He said that was the deal. She had to work for him for one year and then he would pay her way back to Thailand.

Unfortunately, her fights with Khalid increased, and she wasn't treating Nadia very friendly either. I decided not to let her take care of the baby no matter how tired I was.

One day she refused to clean or help with anything. I told her that if she didn't help that Mubarak might not help her get back home. She still refused. The next day Mubarak came home and told me that the maid had given him a letter to mail home, and he had our driver tell us what it said. He said that she put black magic on me and my children to suffer. Mubarak said, "That's bad because the Indonesians are the best people in the world for their witchcraft to succeed." I told him that I didn't believe in that stuff. My faith in God would overrule her witchcraft. He said that I was going to have much suffering and tragedy for the rest of my life because of her curse on me. After that he decided to let her work for his mom. I found out that they didn't like her either and said that she was lazy. Mubarak brought us another maid who was friendly and liked to cook. Mubarak said that this one could stay awhile, but that his mom liked this one because she was a very good cook. Her name was Annie. Annie said that she wanted to stay with me because the Arabs treated their maids like slaves. I told her she could stay as long as she wanted. After I was feeling better Mubarak's mom demanded to have her back and told Mubarak to send the other maid back to Thailand.

Every night Mubarak had to tell me that the maid was going to come in our bedroom and kill us while we slept. At this point it was time for a break from maids and besides, I enjoyed cleaning and cooking. He finally sent her away.

32. The Mutaween

I woke up one morning to the sound of the door banging. Whoever it was didn't want to stop beating on the door. It sounded like more than one man. Then it got louder, and I heard them say in Arabic, " Amerikia joowah". (There is an American inside the house.) I was startled by the knock on the door that led to the neighbor's villa. My neighbor Fatima was yelling and said that she was going to unlock the door. As she opened it she was yelling and motioning me to come up to her villa with the baby. I asked her what was going on. She said there were six men outside the door. She said, "I think they're Mitowahs."(Religious men) They were trying to get in. They were saying that there was an American inside and to kill her. As a chill went through my body, I picked up the baby and ran upstairs with Fatima. As soon as we were upstairs she opened the window and told them to go away that I was a Muslim and to leave me alone. They left after Fatima said that I was a Muslim. She was shaking and told me to stay with her awhile or at least until Mubarak was home. Fatima said she had never seen those men before and was wondering who they were. She said that it didn't look good and told me to stay in the house until she talked to her husband about what had happened. Mubarak wasn't surprised and told me that things were getting worse for Americans in Saudi Arabia. The American Embassies were forbidding Americans to travel to the Middle East. Mubarak said to be careful when I leave the house. He told me to cover my face and eyes when I walk to the shops. Furthermore, Khalid needed to be with me.

Khalid was almost ten years old by then, and his Arabic as well as his English was excellent. It was hard not being able to leave the house. After a week I decided to take a walk with Khalid. Mubarak had taken Nadia and Sarah to visit his mom. I left my eyes uncovered as we walked because there was absolutely no way that I could see through that black material. I was also wearing a pair of jeans which I shouldn't have done, but I was in a state of rebellion after those men came to the house. I was proud to be an American and loved to wear jeans. Khalid put on his white Saudi robe and headscarf. He said he thought that he had better dress like this today instead of wearing pants. I told him that we'll be right back and to just wear his sweat pants, but he said it was just in case. "I said, just in case of what?" He didn't reply. Khalid didn't talk very much as we walked to shops. All he said was that he wanted a schwarma and a strawberry smoothie drink after I was finished. Schwarma's were his favorite food. It was grilled meat and salad wrapped up in fresh pita bread with mayonnaise. I said that would be fine and that I would have one, too. As we walked around the shops Khalid seemed to be on the lookout for something. I told him to look around the shops with me, but he just stood by the door looking outside in the street. He didn't say anything until a man started bothering me in one of the shops. This man wouldn't leave me alone, so Khalid went up to him and said to leave me alone. Khalid said "Let's go to another store." We walked around for awhile without any other incidences until we came to the last shop. I needed to go to the pharmacy to get some medicine for Sarah. I glanced at Khalid who looked worried for some reason and told me to hurry up. I told him that I have never seen him so on edge before and to relax because he was starting to make me nervous. I said, "Cut it out", but he ignored me and stood by the door of the shop while I walked around. Suddenly, a man flung open the door, looked me up and down and grimaced. Then he left. I noticed my jeans were showing, and I had flipped my veil up to read some of the medicine. Khalid looked more nervous and said, "Hurry up, mom." I told Khalid that I wanted to walk around. Khalid was becoming agitated so I said, "Alright I'll hurry." I knew something was going on. Sure enough as I walked out the door two men were shouting, "It's an American, and she's wearing jeans." There were four men, and three were sitting in the car with two of the doors open. One retorted, "Take her and throw her in the car." "She's an atheist." "She worships the devil." I was shocked and just stood there for a moment. Another man said, "Let's take her to jail and let them punish her." Again, they said to the man standing outside of the car to grab me and throw me in the car. My legs wouldn't move. For the first time I was wishing that I couldn't understand Arabic because I couldn't believe what they were saying about me. They didn't even know me. I was wondering where in the world was Khalid when I needed him, but at the time I thought it's better for him to hide and not be seen as the son of an American. Just then the man grabbed my arm and was going to throw me in the back seat of the car when Khalid came running out of the pharmacy with the owner. Khalid jumped in front of me and pulled the man's hand off my arm. He exclaimed, "Leave my mom alone!" "She's a Muslim." "You have no right to say that she's an atheist." The pharmacist was an Arab and started shouting at the men to get away from his shop and to leave me alone or he would call the police. Miraculously, they drove off. The pharmacist asked if I was okay and was mumbling something about stupid mutaween then went back to his shop. Khalid pulled over a taxi and said, "We're going home." I realized my son was growing up at too early an age, but this was his fate-living in the Middle East. Many young boys close to his age were already driving and fighting in wars nearby. I asked him how he knew to be so alert today. He said that his dad told him to take care of me and that he would be in big trouble if he didn't. He said that his dad told him that things weren't very safe for Americans right now. I told him that he definitely earned himself a couple of schwarma's and a smoothie after that courageous bout. I told Mubarak what happened, and he said that I was lucky that Khalid was with me. Otherwise, I would have been kidnapped. He said those men would have raped, killed me, and thrown me in the desert for the buzzards. How dramatic. He said, "It's true, and that's what they do." He forbade me to take anymore walks to the shops. It was too dangerous for now.

I told Mubarak that they had no right to threaten or kidnap me. He said that I have no rights here, especially since I am an American. He said that most of the mutaween hate Americans. They think that if we live here, we will try to change the ways of the Muslims. Especially the younger generation who are ready for a change. They want to wear jeans, drive cars, and not cover their face or eyes. Mubarak reminded me that I am a Muslim now and have to tell people that or I could be killed. "If you're a Muslim you will be protected." I replied," I'm a Christian too, and I do not believe in everything that the Muslims do." I wanted my children to be safe, so I decided to be more stringent with the Muslim ways. I memorized their prayers and got in the habit of praying five times a day. I fasted and memorized more verses from the Qur'an. I finally felt much more confident and was ready if I was ever questioned on the rules or beliefs of Islam.

I started wearing long skirts under my abiyah instead of jeans, but the mutaween still waved their sticks at me when I left my eyes uncovered. I cursed at them behind my abiyah and said to myself that someday I'll be free again. I kept my belief in Christianity to myself for the time being but kept teaching the Bible to Khalid and Nadia in their bedrooms. I kept my Bible, the cross, and a children's Bible hidden in my closet under my clothes. Khalid loved the Bible and the stories-especially Noah and his Ark.

33. The Last Ramadan

It was Ramadan again. This would be my last Ramadan in Saudi Arabia, but of course I didn't know it at the time. I knew how to cook all the special Arabian dishes for Ramadan. The most important was the soup and samboosa. (mutton rolled up in phyllo dough. The lamb bones make a great broth and oatmeal is added after the meat is cooked which makes a very healthy soup.

I knew how to make Arabic cahawa (coffee) and would put that on the floor with the dates. It was tradition to break the fast with dates and drink some Arabic coffee. We would eat on the floor because this is how the Prophet Muhammad would eat, but I would put a long white tablecloth down first before I started putting the plates of food on the cloth.

One night Mubarak had taken the children to their grandma's and grandpa's house to visit. He said that he would be back later to break his fast with me. I finished cooking, so I decided to sit outside on our porch to watch the sunset and wait for the call to prayer. Even though the walls were very high around the house, I could still see the sunset. It was so peaceful watching the orange streaks across the sky fade as the sun slowly went down. It was still very hot outside, but there was a slight breeze blowing. As drops of water dripped down my face from the heat, I looked up into the sky and prayed that someday I would be able to go back to America and live. For some strange reason I asked God to find me an American man who would want to be with me even after living this life in Arabia. I did not want to be surrounded by walls ever again.

As the sun slowly set I prayed that someday soon I would be surrounded by trees and have a swimming pool since I hadn't been able to swim much or at all in thirteen years. I also dreamed of having a beautiful white baby with green eyes and blond hair. Suddenly my dreaming was interrupted by the call to prayer. (Hayah a Salat) Come to pray, Come to pray. It is better for you if you only knew. This is what the Imam (a very religious man or priest) would say at every prayer. The call to prayer brought me back to reality, and I went into the house to get something to eat to break my fast. I was used to the call to prayer and would miss not hearing it anymore. It was something special in a way to know that all the people of the city heard this call to pray to God. Everyone in the entire city would pray at the same time. This seemed like something good for people to do since we should be praying and giving thanks to our creator shouldn't we? For those who believe that there is truly something after this life.

Mubarak was late for breaking his fast. I took a bite out of a fresh date and sipped on some coffee. Then I put my soojed (rug) on the floor to pray. I guess I was becoming a Muslim who believed in Christianity as well. One of my American girlfriends who is married to an Arab said that she was a Jew, Christian, Muslim, and a Buddist. I said, "How can you be all of those?" She said that she believed in all of them. She related to me, "The Jews, Christians, and Muslims believe and pray to the same God as Abraham did." She then told me that she felt that Buddism is also very peaceful.

I just finished praying when Mubarak quietly walked in the door. He said that he was glad to see me praying even when nobody was around. He said that he broke his fast at the mosque and prayed there. Mubarak said that during Ramadan the mosque provides dates for all Muslims to break their fasts.

I brought some soup and samboosa (phyllo filled with meat) and set it on the floor. I was hoping that he couldn't read my mind about how I wanted to leave Saudi Arabia. Of course I cared for him, but we didn't belong together in this world, and I knew it. I'm sure that he knew it too.

A few days later I woke up having a vivid dream. I saw a beautiful white baby with blonde hair and greenish-blue eyes. Then I saw myself sitting in someone's house on the end of a bed looking out a window. I felt that I was very sad at the time that something was wrong. I felt happy and sad at the same time. Then I woke up. The window was made of wood and reminded me of the shape of an old wagon wheel. That's what popped into my head as I saw the window in my dream. I wondered where that window was and thought that it couldn't possibly be in Saudi Arabia because nobody had wooden windows like that.

34. The Christmas Nightmare

When Christmas rolled around I missed home even more. One year I put white lights around one of my plastic trees. Khalid asked if Santa would come. I said that I would try to contact him to see what I could do. I asked Mubarak if we could go to the diplomatic quarters to see Santa. I would get newsletters from the American Embassy that's how I knew what time Santa was coming. He said that we could check it out.

Unfortunately, when we arrived at the Embassy and asked to go inside Mubarak was denied entry. I showed them my American passport, and they said that I could go inside with the children but not Mubarak. I asked if they could make an exception for the children, but they said that they couldn't let Mubarak in without an American passport. Mubarak became very angry and said we had to go which made Khalid and Nadia begin crying. He said the Americans were stupid with their Santa Claus. We got back into the car. As we drove out of the diplomatic quarters, he threw his glass drink at a security guard. It went smack dab into the guard, and was he ever mad. He pulled out his gun and started chasing us out of the gate all the while aiming his gun at us. Then I saw another man running with a gun. Khalid was just staring out the back window- probably in shock. I immediately got up and leaned over my seat and pushed his head down, and Nadia's, as I saw the guards chasing us with guns. Just then I looked up and saw that the second guard raised his gun and was aiming at the car. I put my head down and covered the baby as I heard a shot. We just made it out of the gate. I was shocked at what had happened and that we got away. I was surprised that there were only two security guards chasing us. It must have been because it was Christmas Eve and what idiot would cause a problem on this night except Mubarak.

Mubarak was speeding down the interstate by now, and I knew there was nothing that I could say. I just wanted the children to get home safely. Suddenly, I heard these loud screeching sounds all around us. It sounded as though there was going to be a crash any moment. Mubarak unexpectedly put his breaks on, and we came to a complete stop in the middle of the highway. It was a four-way stop, and there were four cars surrounding us. Each car was approximately four feet from hitting us although one was much closer. There was a car in front, in the rear, and on both sides. All I could think was that we had some fantastic guardian angels among us this night. I saw that Mubarak had gone straight through a red light. We all would have been smashed if those other drivers wouldn't have been so alert. The four drivers were angrily shouting out the window while they slowly backed up. Almost immediately Mubarak went around the cars and took off again. Khalid didn't speak the rest of the night. Actually, none of us spoke a word. Mubarak just kept saying, "Stupid Americans." I quietly said that the guards were not stupid. They had to protect their compound from anyone acting strangely or stupidly drunk and or anyone without an American passport.

I did manage to secretly wrap one gift for Khalid and one for Nadia, the next night. I told them that Santa had made it after all, and that he loved them, too. I let them open their gifts while Mubarak was gone. They never did tell Mubarak that Santa had left each of them a gift.

I tried to stay as positive as I could about all the horrible things that kept happening, and I remembered what one of my Arabian friends had told me once. She said, "The people who God loves the most suffer the most so they won't have to go through any suffering as they pass through the afterlife." "God also puts these people on the highest level of the heaven." I thought that if there are seven levels in the heaven that I should be getting pretty close to one of the top levels by now. Little did I know how much more mental suffering I would be going through and soon.

After another two times of driving with Mubarak and his drunken road rage I'd had enough. One time he was on the interstate speeding and was mad at a driver, so he opened his window and threw a water bottle at the man's front window which immediately splattered. The driver then turned his car toward us. Both men started screaming at each other while driving down the interstate nearly crashing into each other until finally subsiding. The next time Mubarak went up over the median of the interstate almost flipping the car over, but we were lucky again as we landed upright although, somebody from behind almost crashed into us. I told him that I would not get into the car with him anymore while he was drinking. Usually, the day after the incidents he would tell me that he didn't remember what he did and said he was sorry.

Mubarak's drinking increased as well as the staying out at all time of the nights. He would come home at four in the morning. One late night he brought a Moroccan belly dancer home to spend the night. Of course she slept in the living room. That was probably the last "draw" for me, especially when Khalid and Nadia kept asking who she was. I decided that night that I would somehow convince Mubarak to let me go home with the children, and I would never return to Saudi Arabia again.

Nadia, Sarah, and Khalid

35. Planning the Escape

One night when Mubarak was on another heavy drinking binge, he decided to have an argument, I decided to get my suitcase and put it out on the floor. I told him that I wanted to go home since I hadn't seen my parents in a couple of years. My Dad's health was failing as well. I felt that I had a good enough reason to go.

My family hadn't seen Sarah since she was born, and it had been a few years since they had seen Khalid and Nadia. It was next to impossible to ever talk to them on the phone. Mubarak glared at me for a moment. I thought to myself, "Well, this is going to be a no, so I'd better be thinking of another plan pretty fast." To my surprise he said okay. He said maybe I needed to get away. I left my suitcase out hoping to pack within the week.

The next day he called from work and said that he got us our tickets, but that I would have some layovers in London and Greece which I said would be fine. I immediately started packing. Khalid asked if we were going to America. I immediately replied, "Yes, and you will see grandma and grandpa again and watch the fireflies at night." He asked how long we would be staying. My reply was that we would stay as long as possible.

The next day Mubarak seemed to be in a good mood, so I decided to ask him if I could stay in Indiana until Christmas since it had been almost fourteen years since I had been in America at Christmas. I knew he didn't like Christmas, so I threw in that I wanted to see the snow because it had been so long since I was home in the winter or any other season except summer. He said that I would have to find a school for the children to attend. I said that I would. I also told him that I wanted to go back to school. He said that he would think about it. Mubarak's final decision was that we could go for the summer, and he would send our winter clothing in the fall.

I packed as much as I could. I knew Mubarak would become suspicious if I packed my winter clothes. I put a pair of jeans and a sweater or two at the bottom of my suitcase. I wanted to take my beautiful sparkling gold sets that I had gotten through the years, but I knew Mubarak would tell me to keep them here. I also knew that he would look through the closet to see what I had taken. I had to leave all of my tailored silk dresses, fancy shoes, and sparkling gold behind among other cherished items that I wished I could have taken. I decided to keep more room for the children's clothes. Mubarak asked why I was taking so many winter clothes for the children, and I told him some nights were cold. The children would need their sweatshirts and pants to keep warm. He said that he would send me the rest of the clothes in the winter, but I knew otherwise.

I looked around the house for the last time. I would miss our beautiful marble floors. I wouldn't hear the call for prayer anymore. I would also miss that eerie, but peaceful prayer call from the mosque. How strange that I had become so accustomed to the Saudi Arabian lifestyle. This country and its culture would be embellished in my mind forever.

Mubarak came home one night and said that he had my exit visa. I could finally leave. I had to return to Saudi Arabia within the year to be able to ever return again. Otherwise, it would be next to impossible for me to get back into the country again. This was going to be one of my longest trips with all three of the children, and most certainly my last.

36. Leaving for the Last Time

At nine o'clock at night we were on our way to the airport. Khalid was eager to go, Nadia was her happy self as usual without a care in the world, and Sarah was fussing for her bottle and pacifier. Sarah would hold on to me like there was no tomorrow. If ever there was a momma baby, it was definitely Sarah. She acted as though she would die if I was ever out of her sight.

I wasn't looking forward to two days without sleep. I knew Mubarak would make reservations for us that would include long layovers and changing planes in different countries. I was right as I glanced at the tickets he handed me. We were to leave Saudi Arabia on Egyptian Airlines therefore; we went to Egypt first and continued on to Greece where we changed planes after a twelve hour layover.

I waved goodbye to Mubarak and quickly boarded the plane wanting so badly to leave this country forever. This country was my jail that had sheltered me from the real world for almost fourteen years. I was thirty-two years old now and felt that I had lived a lifetime traveling all over the world and meeting so many different people from so many different countries.

I found our seats and got the children settled and pulled off my burgha. I put my burgha in the pocket in front of me and swore to leave it in there as I would exit the plane later on. I left my scarf on so as not to have any problems with any mitowahs (religious extremists such as the Taliban). There was a prayer in Islam before we took off. It said La Allah el Allah (There is only one God). I asked God to keep my children and me safe on our trip.

It was midnight before we were on our way to Greece. When we did land in Greece the nightmare began. We were going to have a fifteen hour layover. I asked to be put in a hotel so my children could rest. I was taken to a hotel, but when I arrived the attendants at the front desk told me that all the rooms were taken. I was exhausted, and Sarah needed her diaper changed. She was crying and wanted a fresh bottle of milk. Khalid and Nadia were fighting and complaining. I laid it on the front desk person that he better get us a room and fast. As I recall, I must have made a scene because I noticed everyone in the lounge looking at me.

I was tired of fighting with this man at the front desk who was telling me that there were no rooms. I told him that I didn't believe him and to give me anything. Finally, he gave in and gave us a room. He said it would be a small room with only two twin beds because that was all that was left. I told him that I would take it.

I carried Sarah while the whining from Khalid and Nadia kept increasing. When we got to the room I put them all in bed. Khalid didn't want to go to sleep. He said, "Mom, I want to go to America." I told him that it was going to take longer than I thought. We had to wait for the next plane to come. I told him to go to sleep and rest for now. I never did sleep. In fact, I stayed awake for almost three days taking only short naps when I couldn't keep my eyes open anymore.

I could never take my eyes off of my children. I loved them so and never wanted any harm to ever come to them.

Finally, we were off to London. After a five hour layover in London, we went to New York. When we got to New York our plane had already taken off for Maryland. I had to call my sister Lisa and tell her that it would be one more day until we would get there.

I had to beg the airlines for a room in New York. I told them that I came from the Middle East and had been traveling for three days, so I refused to sit on some chairs with three children for a whole night and asked for the manager. I said that my children were hungry and tired. Sarah was screaming for a fresh bottle of milk by this time. Nadia was crying, and Khalid was giving the lady behind the counter a dirty look. He said my sisters and my mom need a room. Luckily enough, we were taken to a beautiful hotel and received vouchers to get a really nice meal. I swore to myself that I would never take a trip like that ever again.

37. A New Beginning

The next day we arrived in Maryland to visit my sister Lisa. I never did tell her that I was planning to stay in the States and never go back to Saudi Arabia. I decided that I had better wait and tell her later. We stayed for about a week and then took a flight home to Indiana where my mom met us at the Indianapolis airport. It was good to be "Back home in Indiana."

I couldn't believe that I was thirty-two years old now, but I mentally felt like I was only nineteen, the age when I left home. It had been a long fourteen years living in the Middle East. I felt like a foreigner in my own country. As I walked through the airport I felt as though I should cover my face and hair for fear of being caught and put in jail. I had to remind myself that I was back home in the land of freedom. I was having culture shock back in my own country. Whenever I started talking in Arabic to my children, people would look at me strangely.

I knew it would be hard to start a new life alone with my three children, but I knew I had to try. I stayed at my parent's house for awhile and then lived with my oldest sister and was planning to look for a place to live on my own. One day when I was at my sister's house, she said that we should take the children swimming since they were getting bored. I agreed and she said that we were going to her friend Tim's house, who had a pool. She said that it was her best friend's brother's house. Her name was Renee. She was a good friend of mine as well.

Anyway, we packed the children's things and went to his pool. When we walked in the house, Tim was vacuuming, and I was hoping that we weren't intruding since I was popping in with three children. He turned the vacuum off and said hi and that it was fine for us to go swimming, but he had to go to work.

I remembered now walking in his house when I was eighteen years old. He was just building the house. As I recall, I walked through the living room and thought it was going to be a really neat house. I liked the sunken living room and high ceiling. It just had the wooden frame going up, but I could tell what it would look like. I never did meet him when I was walking through his house at the time. I knew his brother though, two of his sister's, and his mom.

We went swimming a few times at his house, and he was always working so we never saw him much until after two weeks when he finally sat down and talked to us. He was very nice and polite. He had been divorced for about a year, and my sister was helping him with his accounting for his business. They usually just talked about business. I would swim and play with the kids in the pool while they talked.

After a few weeks I moved into a duplex with my children. Mubarak had to call and use his credit card to get us set up in the duplex because I was never allowed to have a checking account or a credit card. I decided that I should open a checking account and put my money there to be safe. I couldn't believe that I had forgotten how to write a check.

I called to have a phone hooked up in our house. The phone company said that I did not exist, and they couldn't help me. I didn't know anybody at the time except for Tim. I called him crying one night and said that I don't exist. I was nonexistent. I asked him if that was even possible. He said that of course I exist; it was just that I never had the chance to build up any kind of credit. I was glad that I existed enough to be able to get furniture and have the television hooked up. The children were excited to finally watch cartoons.

One night I asked Tim if he would come and mow our yard because nobody was coming to mow, or that I would mow it if he would bring a mower. It was overwhelming to have grass to look at instead of sand after almost fourteen years.

The next day when I woke up Khalid said, "Mom, Tim's outside mowing our yard." I thought that was nice of him, although I found it a bit strange that he didn't knock on the door to tell me that he was going to mow. When he was finished and ready to leave, I told him that he could come in for a drink of water. He paused at the door and said some water would be good, but that he didn't want to come in my house and bother me or my children. I gave him a glass of water, and he drank it outside. He left and said that if I needed anything that I could give him a call. I was glad not to be completely alone. Later that night he stopped by again to see how I was doing or if I needed anything else. I said that I was fine and invited him in for supper if he wanted. He said that he had already eaten but said that he would sit out on the porch with me if it was okay. I said I could come out and talk with him for awhile since the children were asleep. I took my monitor with me outside and we sat and talked. It was good to be able to talk with an American man again who seemed to understand me. Although I knew no one would ever understand what kind of life I had lived in Arabia.

The next day I took Khalid and Nadia to their swimming lessons to the same pool that I had taken lessons. Their smiles and giggles proved to me that they were happy. I had never seen them that happy in Saudi. They loved going down the water slide and swimming as well. I would take them to the park after swimming and then to lunch at McDonald's some days. Everything was going very well except one day when we got home the phone rang. I had a terrible feeling in my stomach that it was Mubarak. I unwillingly picked up the phone and it was him. He said that he missed us and couldn't live without us. He said that he changed his mind about letting me stay. He was going to come to America and visit for awhile and take us back home. I said that I wasn't going to go back to Saudi Arabia ever again. The United States is my home, and I'll never leave again. He said that I would change my mind when he arrived. I finally told him that I wanted a divorce, and I was never going back. I wanted to go to college and put the children in school in my hometown. He said that I didn't mean that.

I said that I was never more serious in my life. He became very angry after that and said that he would be getting his ticket soon and would call me when he arrived at the airport for me to pick him up.

This wasn't what I was expecting or was it? I should have known that he wouldn't let us stay here indefinitely. How could I have been so naïve again? I decided that no matter what was going to happen, I would not go back to Saudi.

I decided to call Tim and talk to him about my situation. He asked if I wanted to go have dinner with him, and I said that would be fine because at this point I really needed to talk to somebody for my own sanity. My sister was glad to watch the children for a few hours.

Tim and I went out to a nice restaurant and ordered some soup and a salad which is what I wish we would eat more of these days. He didn't seem to know what to say about my situation, but what normal person would. He talked about other things instead of my problem. I didn't know why he was trying to avoid it, but I didn't want to think about it either, really. Tim was very nice and open minded, and I felt safe with him.

I never remember ever feeling completely safe with Mubarak. I only remember danger always surrounding me.

Tim and I talked very late, and when I got home everybody was asleep. I looked at the light above the sink that my sister left on for me. I never had a light above my sink in Saudi Arabia, nor did I have the dimmer switches. The light in my kitchen in Saudi was only a bulb. It was so quiet and peaceful here listening to the crickets chirping outside. I was home again, and not even the devil, himself, could pull me away from here again. I had made up my mind, and that might not have been a good thing. I didn't like it when I became so stubborn and blocked everything out, but what I wanted and felt that my children needed.

The next day the children wanted to go swimming at Tim's pool, so I said okay. He was working but said that we could swim as long as we liked. Later on he came and swam with the kids and me. Tim would do flips off the board and of course Kelly wanted to learn how to do that, so Tim taught him. Tim took Kelly and Nadia down to a lake next to his house later on in the evening. They went fishing. Both Kelly and Nadia loved going fishing. This was really a new experience for them. Tim gave Kelly his cowboy hat and took him down by the fence to see the cows, too. Kelly was laughing and giggling and telling me about the cows and fishing. I told them that it was getting late, and it was time to go home. I didn't want to stay any longer because I was starting to enjoy Tim's company too much and wasn't ready to have any relationship other than a friend at this time in my life. We said goodbye and went home.

38. He Came to Take Us Back

A few days later Mubarak called and said that he needed to be picked up at the airport. I told the children that their father was here, and we were going to the airport to pick him up.

Mubarak came with his brother Ahmed, which didn't surprise me in the least because the Arabs bring family when they know trouble might arise. He gave the children hugs and said salom a laykoom to me. (Peace be with you) I replied the same in Arabic.

Mubarak and his brother were hungry, so we went out to eat. He acted normal as did I until Khalid said something about Tim. Khalid said, "We met this really nice man, and his name is Tim." (Out of the mouth of babes!) "He mowed our yard, and we went swimming in his pool." Well, of course that set Mubarak off. Arabs don't believe that women should have friendships with other men. It just doesn't happen. I was supposedly a Muslim and wasn't supposed to be around any strange men.

I knew that it would be utterly impossible to tell him that my sister had decided to take us to swim in Tim's pool, and the children really enjoyed swimming.

Anyway, it was my life now, and I wanted a divorce and wanted to live in America. We went home, and I put the kids to bed. Mubarak said that he and his brother were going to take the car and go out for awhile but would be back. I knew exactly where they were going and what they were going to buy. They were going to the liquor store to get whiskey and beer which was next to impossible to get in Saudi Arabia.

They came back late and Mubarak started guzzling the whiskey from the bottle immediately. After half of the bottle was gone, he said that he had changed his mind about my staying in the United States. He said that he would stay for a week or two and then all of us would have to go back to Saudi with him. I told him that I wasn't going back to Saudi Arabia ever again, and my children were staying here with me and I wanted a divorce. He became angry which was understandable and continued to drink the rest of the bottle. I worriedly put the children to bed. Khalid and Nadia asked if they had to go back to Saudi and I said that I wanted to stay here so they could go to school and have more freedom for their future.

The next day turned into another day of arguing with Mubarak about the future of our children. He wasn't going to talk about any other solution but for me to go back to Saudi Arabia. He said that in ten years he might be willing to let me come back to the United States and stay again for a longer period of time when the children would be older. I thought that ten years is a long time to wish for freedom and that it wasn't going to happen to me again. I was not going to be locked up in my house like a jail without any freedom. I wanted my children to learn about the values that I had and my religion too. I just didn't know how to get out of this situation.

I told Mubarak that I was going to stay with my parents for a couple of days. Since he hadn't seen the children for awhile I told him that he should be able to visit with them before he had to go back to Saudi Arabia. My decision was final, and I wasn't going back to Saudi Arabia; so, I felt that he had the right to spend some time with the children. He had Ahmed to help him with the children, and I knew Ahmed would take good care of them if Mubarak kept on drinking. Ahmed didn't drink and was always very good to me and the children. I felt comfortable with him around.

I had never been away from my children for more than a few hours or one night when they went to visit their grandma or grandpa who lived in Saudi Arabia. It was even harder to spend a night without my two year old with me. She was always hanging on me. She was definitely a momma's baby. I knew I wouldn't be able to take more than a night away from my children.

The next morning Mubarak said that he wanted to talk to me alone about the children. He said that he would meet me at a restaurant. I agreed and went to meet him for dinner to talk about the situation. When I met him he decided to give me a diamond ring. He said that since we had been married for almost fourteen years that it was about time for me to finally have a wedding ring. I was thinking that it was a little late for that but took the ring and thought that maybe I'll just give it to Nadia when she gets older and tell her the whole story about what I was going through. Mubarak said that he wanted me to go back to Saudi Arabia with him, but I still refused. As we were leaving the restaurant, he put a dollar bill on the table and said that was the tip for the waitress. I walked to the door, but I saw him still lingering over the table. I saw him take his lighter out of his pocket, and then I saw the dollar bill on fire. He called the waitress an American slut and pushed me out the door and said we are leaving. He pulled me out into the street and said that he would be talking to me later and got in his car and left.

The next morning my son called me from New York. He said that he was getting ready to board Saudi Airlines to go back to Arabia. I asked where the girls were and he said, "They're with me mom, and they're okay." He said that his dad said that they had to go back home. His last words were, "I love you momma." "Please come get us." I told him that I needed to talk to his dad and the phone clicked.

My heart was racing! How could I get to New York before their plane took off? It would be utterly impossible. How could Mubarak not have told me that he was going to take the children? I was now in a panic in a race for time. There wasn't anything that I could do. It was completely out of my hands. I prayed and asked God what should I do? There wasn't an answer for this nightmare. My life was over or would continue to be a nightmare forever without my children. What would Sarah my two year old do when she didn't see me on the plane with her? What beast would take a mother's children away? I had too many thoughts going through my mind. How will I get to see them again? My entry visa into Saudi Arabia was going to expire. I didn't have an exit visa to get out of Saudi Arabia even if I did get into the country. In the Kingdom of Saudi Arabia a woman has to have a husband or male relation to sign for her to enter or exit the country.

39. Without the Children

The days went by, and I tried to call our home phone in Saudi Arabia which seemed to be disconnected. I contacted the American Embassy in Saudi Arabia, and they said there wasn't really anything they could do about the children. I evidently wasn't the only woman whom this had happened to. I would have to wait and make some sort of plan. In the meantime, I decided to move in with Tim who backed my decision to enroll in a University to get my degree in Elementary Education. He took me back and forth to school until he could get me something to drive. I decided that school would keep my mind occupied until I knew what to do next. My plan in the beginning was to go back to school, but it didn't include Tim or to lose my children. It was all so traumatic! It was also one of the hardest ordeals of my life trying to concentrate on my classes with my children always on my mind.

Sometimes I would have to leave in the middle of class. I would go to the bathroom and cry because I missed my children so much. Then I would force myself to go back to class for the future of myself and my children. I knew that I never wanted to be completely dependent on a man again.

I also worked two nights a week teaching English as a second language to adults as well as children. I was lucky at the time that my oldest sister was an English teacher and helped me to get this job for the local community University.

I was very busy, and the money helped because I knew winter was coming and all I had to wear were summer clothes. I never really needed many winter clothes while living in the desert. I knew the winters in Indiana could be harsh and sooner or later I would need a winter coat and warmer shoes. My sandals that I always wore in the desert would have to be replaced by something warmer.

A friend of mine who lived in Saudi Arabia called and said that maybe I could travel to Jordon and go through the desert on camel to get to Saudi Arabia. I would have to hire some men to go with me. It didn't sound very safe to bring the children back that way through the desert. I was a bit leery about this plan and the expense. I did talk to a man who said he would do it for a hundred thousand dollars, but he couldn't guarantee that it would work. We could be caught and killed. There had to be another way!

One night when I was studying Mubarak called and said that he felt badly about the children and wanted to work something out so that I could be with them. I told him that I would live in Bahrain and get a job teaching English to support myself and the children. He said that he might consider that and was thinking that he would marry an Arabian woman and have a new family with her.

I told him that I wouldn't come to Saudi Arabia, but to bring the children to Bahrain, which was only three hours or less from Saudi to the best of my recollection. He tried his best to coax me into going to Saudi Arabia, but I knew that he would lock me up in the house and never allow me to leave the Kingdom ever again. He could also have me killed by stoning me to death or having my head chopped off. This was because my son had told Mubarak that we all went swimming together in Tim's pool. Since I was married to an Arab, I wasn't allowed to be around any strange men, alone. Mubarak had come to his own conclusion that I had planned on being with Tim, which at the time was not true. The children wanted to go swimming everyday, and Tim's pool was close to my sister's house. It also helped from having to pay so much to go to a public pool.

40. Amsterdam

Mubarak said that we could meet at a neutral place. He asked if I would meet him in Amsterdam. I agreed because I knew if I needed to, I could get out and come back home from there. I was glad that I previously had so much experience as a flight attendant and knew about many different countries, their customs, and entry and exit regulations.

Mubarak said that we could stay in Amsterdam for about a week and discuss our situation about the children and decide what to do. Then we could go to Bahrain where he would have his brother, who lived in Dammam, drive the children to Bahrain to be with me. It was only a short drive over a bridge from Dammam to Bahrain.

He said that he would have a ticket waiting for me at the airport. I packed everything that I owned since I was going to live in Bahrain with my children. I would make it work. I knew I had a lot of experience teaching, and there were many job openings for English teachers in the Middle East. I would be with my children, and Mubarak could marry an Arabic woman. The children would also be able to see their father on a regular basis.

There was only one other thing in my way that was bothering me. After Mubarak had left, Tim and I had become good friends, and I knew that I would miss him. It was nice after all these years to have an American friend. I told him that I had to try to work something out to be with my children. I would do anything to get them back in my arms again. Tim seemed very sad and said that he would be around if I needed him. I thought that maybe Tim could come visit us in Bahrain when I became more settled. He was such a country guy that I wondered if he would ever do that. Maybe as time went on I could get enough money saved so there would be a possibility of coming back to Indiana to live with my children. Only time would tell. The only thing on my mind was to get my children back, and then I would worry about where I was going from there.

I hesitantly boarded the plane. My thoughts were becoming foggy. I couldn't decide if this was the right thing to do. I was thirty-two years old and fighting for my life and my children's.

I thought to myself that since Mubarak was so keen on lying, he may not even be in Amsterdam when I arrive. Lying was just a normal way of life for him that I had gotten used to after almost fourteen years. I realized I was taking a huge chance traveling alone to a foreign country. My parents were very concerned as well.

As I fastened my seat belt, I observed the flight attendant as she went through the motions of her routine of safety procedures. I was remembering how I used to be like her, standing in front of a plane full of people going through the same routine. I must have had a lot of confidence when I was nineteen to be a flight attendant.

I suddenly felt like I was losing all of my confidence after losing my children. My mind and soul would be lost forever if I couldn't get them back. I didn't want to think about it. I would have to be positive and strong for now. My faith in God would keep me going and give me strength as usual.

I looked down under my seat and noticed a card sticking out of my purse that Tim had given me before I left. It was very sad. It said that hopefully time will bring me back to him. I wondered what was going to happen to me now— being torn between two completely different worlds. It was midnight now. I decided that I should get some sleep since this was only a five or six hour flight.

When I looked out my window the sun was peaking through the clouds. It was so peaceful flying and watching the clouds go by. The noise and chaos were down below in the other world. That's what I always thought when I was a flight attendant. I was in my own little world up in the sky. I wondered what Mubarak was thinking as he was flying toward Amsterdam.

It was October and the air was cold as the doors to the plane opened. I was glad that I had brought a warm coat to wear. I might need it here at night.

I took a taxi to the hotel where Mubarak was waiting. He said that he had arrived the night before to make sure that we had a place to stay.

Mubarak was waiting for me in the lobby of the hotel. He said ahlan, a salom a lay kum (Welcome, peace be with you). I replied the same in Arabic. He said that he was glad that I came. I followed him to our room and put my bags down. He said that he was going to call the children, and he would let me talk to them. When I talked to Khalid and Nadia, they seemed fine. It made me feel better to hear their voices again.

He said, "Let's get some coffee and talk." I told him that sounded like a good idea. We walked down the street to a coffee shop. There were many people strolling down the street which reminded me a bit of New York, but the buildings looked different. We sat and drank some coffee. He said he was taking off work this week for a vacation to be with me. He told me not to worry about the children. They were with his parents, and I would soon be able to see them. He said that we might as well go sight-seeing while we were here and make the best of it.

I had never been to Amsterdam before and remembered that Anne Frank's house was here. I decided that I would ask Mubarak if he would want to take a walk one day to find it even though I presumed that he didn't know who she was. He said that would be fine. He thought he remembered reading about her when he was younger.

There were some boats that were giving tours so we boarded one and were taken down a beautiful river. I remember the leaves were falling from the trees. It was very tranquil being on the boat. I was at peace for now thinking that I was getting a step closer to my children. Mubarak seemed to be very relaxed about our situation for now. He said that he didn't want to talk about divorce at the moment. He said, "We need to enjoy this time together." I decided not to analyze what that meant.

Our boat stopped right at the front of Anne Frank's house. I was expecting it to be different. The house was very high and connected to many other houses down the street. It gave me the chills as I walked in remembering reading about her so many times. I often visualized what her house looked like. I tried to soak everything in as I walked through the rooms of the house. As I recall the rooms were quite large with wallpaper falling off the walls. The tour guide said this is where she and her family lived before they went into hiding. Then I asked where their hiding place was. He took us to some steps that we had to walk up. It looked like we were going up into an attic. He said that these steps folded up into the ceiling so the Nazis couldn't find Anne and her family. As I walked up the last step I saw a huge room with wooden floors. It looked like somebody had hammered long planks of wood over the walls and windows. My guess was so that the Nazis didn't think there was a room up this high. It was a good hiding place, and the attic blended in with the ceiling; so, it would have been hard to tell there was a room above. I'm sure they had to be very quiet at times. How sad to think about a girl so young to have to be locked up unable to go outside and play. She was so courageous. I thought that I was really lucky so far to have seen so much in my life and to get through it. She had been locked up in her home more than I had been in Saudi Arabia.

I told Mubarak thanks for letting me go to see her house. He said that it was just a house, and they were Jews. That's why they were killed. It hadn't really occurred to me until now how much the Arabs hated the Jews. That was a scary thought at the moment standing by a Jew hater as I left her house. Mubarak probably thought that it was a good thing to get rid of Anne Frank and her family. I was walking around with a Nazi. This made me think even more that I needed to divorce him and talk about it. Mubarak and I were such different people with our religious beliefs and everything. He needed to be with his own people, and I needed to be with mine.

It had been a long day, and I was tired so we grabbed a sandwich on the way to the hotel. Mubarak ordered a bottle of whiskey to drink in the room. I sat in a chair and read a magazine. He said that he was going out for awhile which was fine with me. I had a stupid idea in my head, that maybe I should call Tim to keep in touch with him, and tell him that I made it to Amsterdam safely. He told me to call him, so why not. I called him and said that I was going to ask Mubarak to divorce me while I'm here and try to get my children, then bring them back to the states, but I didn't know how I would survive. Tim said that he would take care of me and my three children if it needed to be that way. Who would have such a big heart to do such a thing? I told him that Mubarak was drinking heavily and was acting a bit strange, but that I'd have to stick to his plan for awhile to get my children back.

Mubarak came back after an hour and asked if I had called anybody? Afraid to answer at first, I asked why? He said that the front desk said that somebody from our room had called the United States. I decided that I didn't want to get into an argument tonight and would tell him that I called Tim tomorrow. I said that I called my mom to tell her that I was okay. He didn't reply. He continued to drink his bottle of whiskey straight in a glass on ice and smoke continuously. I asked him if I could open a window and he said okay. The smoke was making me sick. I forgot how much he smoked, and it seemed that he was smoking more than ever before. He drank over half the bottle and went to bed and passed out. I made a bed on the floor with some blankets and pillows swearing to myself that I would never lie in bed with him again. I hated myself for hating somebody, but I was really starting to hate him. I knew I would have to keep my feelings to myself and be a good actress to try and get my children back.

The next morning the sun was shining through the windows. It was a beautiful country. I looked outside the window and saw the river, but the street was very quiet. Mubarak said that Amsterdam was more into the night life. He would take me around and show me some places to go tonight. He said that he wanted to sleep a bit longer. I was full of sleep and decided to take a walk. I went to get some coffee and took a walk. It was ten in the morning, and nobody was out and about yet. Many of the shops were closed as well, so I decided to go back to the hotel. I bought a newspaper and decided to sit in the lobby to read for awhile.

Surprisingly enough I looked up to see Mubarak walking toward me. He asked if I wanted to get some lunch. We walked to a restaurant that was just opening for lunch. "The restaurants open late around here," I mumbled. He nodded as he was smoking his cigarette and said most of them don't open up until about three in the afternoon, but they stay open late. He said he was here one whole day before I came so that's how he knew. Ah, he had scoped the place out before I came which was interesting. I was wondering how he knew where to go and what to do. Sneaky as usual!

He said that we could take a train ride to go see the windmills and a winery. We meandered to the train station and paid for our tickets. I noticed that he wasn't talking much today. Something was up!

He said that I was lucky to see this country and get to travel as much as I have. I said I was lucky in some ways to have had such an opportunity to travel but not without my children. He said that we would talk about it later.

The scenery was beautiful! There were a lot of plateaus and sheep around the countryside. I was missing the United States though and said that my country has a lot of greenery and sheep, too. The landscape was nothing out of the ordinary to me.

Mubarak asked me what was wrong. I said that I miss my children and my country. He said that we would talk about it tonight. After the train ride we walked through some museums which was interesting as well, but not what I had in mind. We went into a dungeon which was really creepy. The tour guide talked mostly about the ways people had been tortured a long time ago for being witches or for crimes that had been committed. This made me think about Saudi Arabia and how people's heads and hands were being chopped off and women were still being stoned to death. I needed some air, so I told Mubarak that I wanted to leave. He questioned, "Why, don't you like the museum?" I told him, "No, it's one of the creepiest and morbid museums I have ever seen."

He said that maybe I needed to go to a nightclub later and relax. We took a walk down some different dark and creepy alleys and stopped at a restaurant to have some dinner. Then we walked down some more old, brick covered alleys where the nightlife was evidently just starting. I definitely wasn't prepared for what I was seeing. I guess this is what they called the red light district. There were endless nightclubs with people holding their mugs, singing in what sounded like Dutch or Irish all the while dancing on top of tables. It was a sight that I hadn't seen anywhere before. Everybody was definitely having a good time and nobody was stopping them from dancing and jumping on the picnic table outside.

I wondered as I looked in the windows of all the shops if the parents who lived here let their children walk past these shops because absolutely nothing was appropriate for anybody under the age of twenty-one.

The later it got, and the further we walked down this dimly lit creepy alley, the worse it got. Mubarak said that I had better never walk down this alley alone because I could be killed or kidnapped. Now I know why they call it the red, or blue light district or whatever it's called because there were red and blue lights in the windows with women sitting on chairs in front of the windows. After I saw that I was ready to turn around and get out of this area. Mubarak wanted to go into a nightclub, but I didn't want to dance at that time or with him. Then we went to another nightclub that was a little more relaxing. We talked for awhile and went back to the hotel. Mubarak passed out again when we got to the room. I went to sleep in a chair next to the open window desperately needing fresh air. I was done walking around Amsterdam with Mubarak. Tomorrow it was time to talk business.

I got up early while Mubarak was still sleeping, got some breakfast, and took a walk. It seemed colder this morning, and I felt a chill go up my spine. My intuition was kicking in again. I knew something was going to happen, and it wasn't going to be good.

I walked around until noon before I went back to the hotel. Mubarak was just getting up and was already starting on his whiskey and smoking. I knew today was the day. Then suddenly he asked if I was ready to go back to Riyadh, Saudi Arabia. I said, "I'm not going to let you trick me into going in a country that I know I can never get of out unless you sign for me to be able to leave." I told him that I did not want to be locked up for the rest of my life. I said that I want a divorce and that's final! I'll go as far as Bahrain, and I want the children to be brought to me there.

By this time I knew he was getting angry and asked about the phone call that I had made. He said that he knew that wasn't to my mom and dad's house. I said that I had called Tim to let him know that I was okay. He was worried about me traveling all the way to Amsterdam alone to be here with you.

Then he told me that I couldn't leave him and that he wouldn't divorce me. It was all up to him. He said, "I've the cards in my hands." He said that he could have me stoned to death in Saudi. Whoops! That was the wrong thing to say to me. "Why would you have me stoned because I made some friends in America and got my freedom back?"

I took a deep breath and replied, "I am going to say this one more time." "I am not stupid, and I know your country now inside and out." "I will not step foot in Saudi Arabia as long as I live on this earth, so you better make sure our flight is ready to go to Bahrain as of today." Quietly, he said, "I will die for you and slit my wrists for you so you won't leave me." "If I slit them the wrong way I'll die, and if I slit them another way I could bleed to death if you don't get help for me." This was getting a bit dramatic by now, and I knew he had too much to drink.   I said that I'm taking my bags and going to the lobby. As I turned my back I heard a glass break, and before I knew it he had slit both of his wrists. This was not happening or was it? The blood had poured out of his wrists so fast that the carpet was already a pool of blood. I had only turned my head for a few seconds. I looked at him as though he was a stranger and for a split second the dark side of me took over. "Should I run away and let him die?" Then I could get my children back much easier. Suddenly, Mubarak fell over on the floor. The blood just kept pouring out. I had to think and fast. I picked up the phone and called the lobby. "I need help and an ambulance fast. My husband just slit his wrists and is bleeding to death." The man at the front desk said that he would send somebody right away. There was more blood pouring out of his wrists, I grabbed some towels from the bathroom and tied one around each wrist and put pressure on them. The next thing I remember was that three emergency medical technicians suddenly came into the room and just in time because I thought I was going to faint. The smell of whiskey and blood wasn't going well with my stomach for the moment along with the stress of trying to get my children back.

They put Mubarak on a stretcher and took him to the lobby and than into the ambulance. One of the emergency technicians motioned me to sit up front with him. He asked me what happened. Trying to answer with some sort of sanity I replied, "He wants me to go back to Riyadh with him." The EMT told me not to go back there. He said you will never get out, and after this he will probably have you killed when you get there. Both of the emergency technicians said that I had better watch my back from here on out. They said that I should try to save my life, or I wouldn't be able to take care of my children later on, if I got myself killed.

I thought that I was in a nightmare and couldn't get out of it. How did these men know what Saudi Arabia was like? Furthermore, they didn't even know my life or Mubarak's. The whole situation was bizarre.

When we got to the hospital I ran to the bathroom to throw some cold water on my face. Then I reluctantly went to the emergency room to check on Mubarak. One of the doctors told me that Mubarak needed to pay them somehow. I asked Mubarak to pay them, and he told me to get his credit card out of his wallet. I gave his credit card to the doctor. The doctor gave me a strange look and said that he hadn't signed his name on his credit card. I thought to myself, "Oh no, it's back to the credit card nightmare again". I told Mubarak that he had to sign his name on the credit card to make it legal. He refused to sign it. I told him that they won't be able to continue helping if it isn't signed. I gave him a pen and retorted, "Sign it". Thankfully, he gave in. We stayed for awhile, and the doctor said that he would be okay. The doctor motioned for me to come to his office and then quietly told me that if he really wanted to kill himself, he would have slit his wrists the other way. Evidently, your husband knew what he was doing. The doctor said that after talking to Mubarak his impression was that he just wanted to get my attention. He said that I had better be careful. Why was everybody telling me to be careful? Mubarak was the crazy one trying to kill himself. I thought to myself that maybe I better watch my back from here on out traveling by myself with a possible psychotic Arab.

When we arrived back at our hotel the front desk had our bags out and ready to go. They said that they didn't want Mubarak staying at their hotel anymore. He started fighting with them, and we almost got thrown out. I was already standing outside the door, in the rain, getting soaked watching him argue again as usual. The fresh air felt good, and I didn't even care at this point about getting wet. I was getting cold though. The weather just kept changing. It was getting colder and colder or was it just me and the way I was feeling? Mubarak finally came out of the hotel and said we had to go someplace else for the night. We finally found a different hotel to stay in for one more night. Mubarak got on the phone and made sure our reservations for Bahrain were confirmed for the next morning. He ordered a drink and went to bed. I couldn't believe I had to go through another night here, but we were leaving in the morning. I was grateful for that.

I woke up before him again and looked out of the window. Amsterdam might be a good place to go for a vacation under other circumstances. I just wanted to get to Bahrain and see my children, but was I really going to get to see them?

Mubarak got up and acted like nothing had happened. There was some dried blood on his bandages that made me think of the day before. He said, "Let's have some breakfast, and then we will go".

We took a taxi to the airport. Mubarak never said a word the whole way, and I had nothing to say either. The stained bloody bandage appeared as he raised his hand to his mouth smoking a cigarette. He seemed oblivious to anyone who was staring at his bandages. I knew he was thinking of a plan on how to get me into Saudi Arabia.

Amsterdam

41. Bahrain

The flight from Amsterdam to Bahrain seemed like it took forever. Mubarak didn't say much. He watched a movie and kept laughing. How could he be so happy? It was scary. I was overly stressed and feeling disoriented from a lack of sleep. I was getting closer to his territory, but it helped to know that I wasn't going to Saudi Arabia. Since I had the advantage of being a flight attendant, I knew Bahrain had more freedom for women, and there was an American Embassy around if I needed help. I also knew that the Arabian men in Bahrain were more open minded than the Saudi men; however, there are some Saudi men who are open minded too but very few at that. I was hoping I wasn't going to need any help. He already tried to kill himself. How much worse could it get?

I've discovered when you're going through a traumatic experience; time doesn't seem to matter much. I don't even remember what time we arrived in Bahrain. I remember the taxi driver passing by the beach. Mubarak pointed to the bridge that would take us into Saudi Arabia. He said that he could get me in even though my passport had expired. I would have to keep my face covered, and since I was his wife he thought that we could possibly get through security. There was a chance that they would take me to jail without an entry visa. He then said that it would only take him a couple of days to renew my visa. I said, "How many times have I told you that I'm not going into the Kingdom of Saudi Arabia. I know that for the rest of my life, I will never be able to

185

get out." He was quiet. He said that I was right. He wouldn't let me out for awhile but maybe not forever. He smirked. I turned my head away to think. Should I take a chance and be killed or should I save my life for my children's future?

We went to a hotel and got a room and then went to a restaurant in a hotel to get dinner. He said that he would order warg al aynub and hummus, and lebnah because they were my favorite Arabian appetizers. Warg all aynub was rice with nuts and spices along with other ingredients wrapped up in grape leaves. It was really a Lebanese appetizer. We sat and ate and argued about the children. A strange man came and sat with us, and Mubarak offered him to eat with us. This was a normal custom in Arabia— when strangers come, sit, and eat with other strangers. He told us not to fight because if we get a divorce then for the rest of our lives we will end up trying to kidnap our children back and forth from each other. He said that this would not be good for the children. I told him that he did not understand. He insisted that he did. He said that he knew of a couple in our same situation, and that is what they did for years. Nobody wins!

I thought that sounded very sad. Mubarak and I headed back to our rooms arguing all the way. The argument was escalating, so I backed off afraid that he would do something out of the ordinary as before.

We went to our rooms and he called his brother Ali in Dammam. I heard his brother talking, but Mubarak took the phone away from me. He said that Ali would bring the children.

I went to sleep on the floor again for another night. I was, to say the least, getting tired of sleeping on the floor while Mubarak had a comfortable bed to sleep in but being stubborn and refusing to ever be in the same bed with him ever again, I chose the floor. I woke up and went outside to sit on the balcony and saw the most beautiful sunrise looking over a beach, but all I could think of was to be back in America. I had been to so many places around the world, but the United States was and always will be my home. I missed Christmas and Halloween and every other holiday. I missed being able to vote. Women don't have any rights to speak out or vote in Saudi Arabia. It just was not home in the Middle East. It was a jail! I could be pushed only so far, and I knew it was time to fight back. That I did!

When Mubarak woke up he called for his shahee (tea) and breakfast, and then he came over to talk to me. I was still sitting on the balcony. I was sitting on the cold concrete of the balcony because there weren't any chairs to sit on. I was so used to sitting on the floor for so many years now that it didn't bother me in the least. I stared at the serene blue pool below me that was surrounded by palm trees. I had no desire to go for a swim as good a swimmer as I am. I remembered that my mom had insisted that I go through every level in swimming lessons that were offered. I took enough lessons to be a lifeguard.

Mubarak asked me what was wrong and asked me again if I was ready to go back to Saudi Arabia. I told him that as I long as I live, I will not go back to that country to be his prisoner anymore.

I reminded him that I wanted a divorce and knew that in the Islamic religion that he only had to say it three times, and it would be legal. He evidently changed his mind about breakfast as I saw him pour some whiskey in a glass over ice. I told him that I was going to go for a walk outside and go sight-seeing. I grabbed my camera and went down to the lobby to find a phone. I had a feeling that something was going to escalate and soon. I didn't know who to call for help. I called Tim and my oldest sister. They said that I was crazy of course, to have traveled to Bahrain with Mubarak. I knew that, but that was beside the point now. My oldest sister said that I shouldn't go into Saudi Arabia because Mubarak will never let me out. I told her I had to hang up because he was coming.

Just then Mubarak walked into the lobby, grabbed the phone, and hung it up. He said, "I know who you're calling." "Nobody in America can help you here." "The cards are in my hands." He was wearing his Saudi dress and scarf. He had that crazy look in his eyes again as he did when he was going to do something violent. His eyes were bloodshot red. He said if he had to he would have me kidnapped and taken back to Saudi Arabia. He said that there were some men coming to do exactly that if I wouldn't cooperate. He then retorted, "If you don't believe me, just look outside the door."

At this time we were both standing in the middle of the lobby. The front desk attendants were staring at both of us. They asked if I was okay. I looked out of the door, and sure enough there were three men getting out of the car heading straight for me. Mubarak was on his cell phone talking in Arabic. I heard him say, "That's her. Take her." I froze. I didn't know which way to go. They would eventually catch me if I ran outside. He had this planned all along. Mubarak was standing right in front of me. He ripped my camera out of my hands, and threw it on the floor. Then he picked it up and smashed it against the wall. I asked him why he had to break my camera, I asked, "Why do you always have to break things?" I realized there wasn't time to argue about the most expensive camera that I had ever owned in my life. I had to think fast. I told Mubarak that I would get in the car with the men, but that I needed to tell the front desk to get my bags. By this time some Arabic men came over to Mubarak and asked him why he was bothering me. I told the men in Arabic that he was bothering me. I knew this would buy me some time. I slowly crept backward. Mubarak started yelling at the men to mind their own business. Then all of them were yelling and shouting in Arabic at each other. Suddenly Mubarak hit one of the men which caused an all out fight. The other men were yelling at Mubarak and grabbing his arm. This was good. It would buy me some time. I ran to the front desk, grabbed a pen and wrote Tim's number down. I told Vernard, the front desk attendant that there were some Saudi men who were trying to kidnap me and take me to Saudi Arabia. I told him to call this man. He was an American, and I needed his help right away. Vernard got on the phone as I was standing there and called Tim. Vernard handed me the phone. I told Tim what was going on as I watched Mubarak start swinging his arms at the men. The other three men that were supposed to kidnap me were coming closer. I told Tim I had to go. As I glanced over my shoulder, I saw Mubarak walking toward the front desk. I gasped and dropped the phone. As soon as I dropped the phone Mubarak picked it up and told Tim that he was an American white devil. Mubarak said that he was a constituent and there was nothing that Tim could do to help me and hung up the phone. Tim called Vernard again and told him that there is an American woman in serious trouble, and I am an American man and will be responsible for whatever it takes. He told Vernard to get me a bodyguard immediately. After Mubarak hung up the phone I ran. I headed straight to the elevators. Thank God it was a huge hotel where I could hide if I needed. First, I needed to get to my room to get some of my things. Before I started running, I quickly glanced back.

The crowd was moving toward Mubarak. Our eyes locked through the crowd, and he started running toward me. I had to move and fast. I knew he was right behind me. I ran so fast that I slid through the hall but made it to the elevator and pushed the button. As it was closing I saw his hands trying to pry the doors apart. I felt the adrenalin flowing through my veins. Trembling, I pushed the button again and hit his hands as hard as I could! The door closed. I made it! It seemed only seconds when the door opened to the second floor. I looked around, took a deep breath and ran to my room and grabbed my bags which I had never unpacked. This was stupid. I could never get out of here alive! As I was going out the door, Mubarak was standing there. I told him to leave me alone that security would be coming, and he didn't need that. He grabbed my purse, but I had already taken everything out of it knowing that would be the first thing he would grab. I started backing up into the room. He threw my purse against the wall. Then he grabbed a glass and threw it right at my face. I ducked as pieces of glass went flying everywhere. Then he took a long swing at me with his fist. I ducked again, and he fell against the wall. His balance was always off after he drank whisky, and I knew that. This was my only advantage. Just as he was coming at me full force with his body, two men entered the room and jumped in front of Mubarak. The men asked what was going on.

Mubarak backed up and asked if I still wanted a divorce, and I told him, yes. Mubarak said, Then all I have to do is say that I divorce you three times. I said, "Go ahead and say it." "We have two witnesses now and that's what I need." He said, "I divorce you, I divorce you, I divorce you." I replied, "That's it?" He said, "Yes, we're divorced." Then he remarked that he could marry me again later on. Shocked, I said, "I don't think so." The two men were security, and they told Mubarak that he had to go with them. It was too late. Mubarak pushed both of them and dashed down the hall. The security guards told me to lock my door, and they would be back. I shut the door and locked it. I put a table against the door, and then a chair and anything else I could push over to block the door. Only a few minutes passed, and there was a banging on the door. I wasn't about to open it for fear it was either Mubarak or the three men who he had gotten to kidnap me. Somebody knocked again. Suddenly a man yelled and said that he was my bodyguard. An

American man named Tim said that I needed him. My hands were shaking. He said to look through the peek hole, and I would see his badge. I squinted as I looked through the hole. I decided to take a chance by opening the door. This guy was huge and tall. He was at least six foot five and as big as Arnold Schwarzenegger. I was shocked. I had never seen an Arab so tall and muscular before. He told me to get my bags and go with him. I needed to get to another room quickly because Mubarak's men knew where I was. As we walked I noticed there was construction going on, but we kept going. This was a huge hotel! I decided to ask this man who had asked for a bodyguard for me. He said that my friend the American man named Tim told Vernard to get me one. Tim was trying to be Bruce Willis long distance. I had to admit he was doing a good job so far!

We finally arrived to another room. He said that I should be safe here for awhile. He went into the room first and walked around. Suddenly the phone rang. I said, "It's Mubarak. He knows that I changed rooms." The bodyguard told me to pick up the phone. Sure enough it was Mubarak. He said that I won't get away. He would find me wherever I go. I slammed the phone down. I told my bodyguard that we had to move again and fast. Mubarak was coming. We quickly went to another room. This room was on the very top floor. It was getting late by now, and I was getting tired of running. My bodyguard checked out the room and said that he would stand outside the door to make sure that I would stay safe. He told me that I would be okay and to try to get some sleep. Since it was getting so late Mubarak would probably wait until morning to try another plan.

I called my mom to tell her what was going on. She said that I needed to get out of there and come back to the United States. She said that I had better be careful and not to go into Saudi Arabia. She advised me to call the American Embassy and ask them to escort me to the airport. She would pay for the ticket home.

Next, I called Tim and told him what was happening as well. He said that he would pay for my ticket as well to get me back home safely. I said that I would call him in the morning. I thought that I was lucky to have family and friends because some women in my situation don't have either.

It was hard to sleep, of course, with my life being in danger, but I felt better knowing that there was a bodyguard outside my door with security nearby as well. All I could think about was how to get my children. I needed to call the American Embassy here in Bahrain for immediate assistance. I decided to take a nap first and finally dozed off.

The phone woke me up. It was Mubarak again. He said, "I told you that I would find you." He said that I would never escape. He said he had decided to let me get some sleep and maybe when I woke up that I would come back with him to Saudi Arabia. I hung up the phone. I looked out my door and my bodyguard was still there, so I opened it and told him that Mubarak had just called. The bodyguard told me that the Bahraini police were coming to help me.

The phone rang again. I answered. It was Mubarak again, so I hung up. As I was getting dressed there was a faint knock on the door. It was my bodyguard carrying a tray. He told me to eat some breakfast. He said it's going to be a long day for me. I told him thanks. After I ate there was a knock on the door again. It was a Bahraini policeman. He said that he wanted to ask me a few questions. His name was Khalid, my son's name. Khalid told me that he had the hotel surrounded with police all night up until now. So that's why Mubarak didn't come to my room.

I pulled back the curtain and looked out the window. There were police cars everywhere. They were lined up in a row with their lights flashing. There must have been over fifty cars down there. The hotel was definitely surrounded. I thought this would make a great movie if I survive to tell it.

Khalid spoke English very well and was very polite. He said that the Saudi men can be crazy. He said that they would have kidnapped me if I hadn't run or called security. I was very lucky and would probably have been killed by the Saudi men. Khalid said that there were four men with Mubarak. He asked if I knew who they were. I said that I had never seen any of them before. Khalid said, "The Saudi men have no hearts." Evidently many women come to Bahrain to escape their Saudi husbands to no avail. I heard one Saudi man threw his wife out of the car while he was still driving. He snatched her baby from her arms before he threw her out of the car. This woman said she never saw her baby again. The Islamic religion says that a baby is to be with the mother especially while the mother is nursing. When the baby becomes four or five the father will take him or her if the mother remarries or if the father chooses.

It unfortunately sounds like there are some Saudi's who aren't living by the laws of Islam or by the Hadith's of the prophet Muhammad. However, my Saudi sister-in-law, named Fatima, had divorced her husband after he decided to marry another woman. She kept her little boy. She also turned down many future husbands, so she wouldn't lose her son upon remarrying. She chose to live with her mother who also helped raise Fatima's son.

I told the policeman that Mubarak had called a short while ago. The policeman said that Mubarak and the men with him wouldn't be able to get through with the hotel being surrounded.

Khalid told me what I had to do next. He said he would keep the hotel surrounded. I would leave at the back of the hotel. There would be a bodyguard who would follow me to the back parking lot of the hotel. There would be three men waiting in a car who would take me to the American Embassy. I would be safe there until a flight would be available back to the United States.

Khalid asked if I was ready to go. The bodyguard followed me as I walked down the hall. It seemed like forever until we got to the back of the hotel. The bodyguard stopped as we reached the outside door. He opened the door and told me to walk down to the parking lot and there would be three men waiting in a car to take me to the Embassy. He said that they would be dressed in street clothes so they wouldn't be noticed by anyone.

I looked around, and it was very quiet. It was too quiet. I wondered why the bodyguard couldn't follow me out to the parking lot. What if this was a set up, and the three men ended up being some of Mubarak's men. I would have to chance it and put my trust in Khalid, the Bahraini policeman. I was suddenly feeling the lack of sleep affecting my body. I felt dizzy as I picked up my suitcase and wearily began walking down the sidewalk. I saw the three men waiting in a white car. One got out and helped me with my suitcase, and told me to get in the backseat. He told me to hold on because he was going to drive fast. I guess he wanted to get out of the parking lot as quickly as possible. As we came out from the back of the hotel, there were still police cars surrounding the building. I wondered where Mubarak had gone. Was he still lurking around? The three men told me not to worry that they would get me to the American Embassy.

When we got on the highway I saw the bridge that kept me getting to my children. I wanted to get out and run to the bridge. I thought that maybe I could swim across, but I remembered this bridge when I was a flight attendant. All the flight attendants looked out the windows and saw massive packs of sharks below. I knew the sharks were there. I wouldn't make it across swimming. I asked the three men if they could take me across the bridge. They said that the Saudi police would put me in jail because I was an American without a legal entry visa to get in. They said that the Saudi checkpoint would never let me through. I would be putting my life in danger. They said it wasn't worth it. My only hope would be to see if the American Embassy could help.

The men dropped me off. I was alone again in another foreign country, but I was glad to be at the American Embassy. I walked to the gate waiting for somebody to open the doors. The gate was ten to twelve feet high. Someone came and asked to see my American passport then suddenly the huge metal black doors opened. It was a beautiful Embassy. The floors were made of brown speckled smooth marble and very high ceilings. I thankfully walked into the consulate's office. A lady took me to talk to the consulate. He was very polite and understanding. He said they have had many American women in my situation come to the Embassy seeking safety from a Saudi husband. He gave me a plane ticket, but said that I would have to spend the night at the Embassy. I couldn't be protected if I left.

The lady took me to a lounge. She said that I could walk around if I wanted. She would come back in the morning to escort me to the airport. There was an American military man keeping watch for the nights, so I had somebody to talk to. When I saw him in his uniform I started crying. He asked me what was wrong. I said that I missed my country and my people. I never wanted to come back to Arabia ever again after all that has happened to me. He told me that I could walk with him while he did his night patrolling. We walked up and down the Embassy together and talked. He asked where I was from. I told him Indiana. He said that he was from Montana. I told him that I never wanted to see another Arab. He said, "That's understandable. There are many nice American men." I told him that I knew someone who is a real country boy and redneck and who is trying to help me get back home. The guard quipped that he was a redneck, and there's nothing wrong with that. I forgot this military man's name, but he went to get us some dinner. We sat and ate together then I rested until the lady that worked with the consulate came and took me to the airport.

I don't remember her name, but she had black hair and was short and stocky. I told her it might be a good idea for us to have a gun just in case Mubarak and some of his people would be waiting at the airport. Suddenly she pulled a gun out of her pocket. I said, "Good. I'll take one too if you've got another one." She said that when we get to the airport, she would give me one.

We didn't have any problems getting to the airport. She talked to me for awhile. She said to keep in touch with her to see what we could do about my children. She said that if I could figure out a way to get them back that I would have to go in hiding maybe for the rest of my life. He would keep coming back to kidnap them. I was stressed to say the least when I got to the airport. The consulate gave me a small handgun. I pondered at the thought if I would really shoot somebody or not. I suppose I would if Mubarak or somebody would try to take me. I was glad I had it. She said, It's loaded so be careful. You can have it until you board the plane." It worried me a bit that she even had a gun. She must have heard what happened and might have been worried that some of Mubarak's people were there, whoever they were. We walked through the airport without any problems and continued walking to where the passengers were boarding. She said that I should be okay for now. I told her thanks and that I would keep in touch with her about the children.

42. Back Home Alone

I t was the longest flight back home that I had ever had. I was glad that I was a flight attendant because I was used to such long delays and the flying. I had to wait seven hours in London. I sat down in a chair while I waited at the airport, and the tears would uncontrollably flow as I thought about my children and all that had happened. I made myself get up and walk around. I hadn't slept in two days or was it more? Time wasn't important right now. I had to be strong and keep going. I still had my life and was young enough to start over if I had to.

I was so glad to be out of the Middle East and knew that I would never return except to try and get my children back again if I would ever make the attempt again.

I finally arrived back in Indiana, but as soon as I got off the plane I had this horrible, lonely, eerie feeling. My children were not with me! How would I ever be able to live the rest of my life without them? Would it be possible?

Tim was waiting for me at the airport. He was smiling and asked if I had eaten. I said not much so he took me to the Olive Garden to get something to eat. He told me that I could stay with him if I wanted until I decided what I wanted to do. I didn't think I had many options at this point. I didn't have any money since Mubarak had everything that I ever made or had.

Winter was coming in a couple of months, and I didn't have any winter clothes after living in the desert for so long. I only had my desert sandals which is what I called my shoes. I guess I would just freeze to death. Why were these morbid thoughts going through my head during that time? Tim told me not to worry that he would buy me a coat, and I wouldn't freeze to death.

I knew that my parents would like me to live at home, and they would help me, but I felt that I shouldn't at this time in my life. Or was the real reason because I really liked Tim and wanted to be with him? Of course, being a parent myself, I knew my parents would end up helping me as much as they could, which they did as usual.

The days went by, and I called the American Embassy in Riyadh to help me. They said there wasn't much they could do to get my children back. Saudi was the only country in the world where women don't have any rights at all. They said that they could check to see if the children were okay, but they couldn't take them away from a Saudi. It would cause too many political problems from what I understood.

Next, I talked to an American married to a Saudi who moved to the United States. She said that her husband could give me a map that would take me through Jordon and then to Saudi Arabia. I would have to travel by camel. I would fly to Jordon and hire some men to go with me on the trip. It would take a few days traveling through the hottest desert in the world. Her husband said it could be possible, but I could also be shot and killed or die from being lost in the desert. Then I would have to take the children back the same way. My children were too small to go through those conditions. My son might be okay, but I didn't know if I wanted to take the chance for him to be hurt. I also promised my children that no matter what happens to me that I wanted them to stay together and take care of each other. I know that I could never just take Khalid and not my two daughters. If I could get to them I would take them, too.

Tim told me that I would be crazy to go through the desert to get my children. He said that I would be killed. My mom and dad were against the idea as well. Coincidently, my mom was working for the State Department at that time and made calls to international lawyers whom she knew. She also discussed the situation with a retired army intelligence officer. All her contacts related that it would cost a lot of money to hire someone to get the children out of Saudi Arabia. They all stated that the children would most certainly be kidnapped later according to what mom told them about Mubarak's actions and what they knew about the Saudi culture.

I decided to check on the Internet to see if there was someone who could help me. I found that there were many women in my situation who had lost their children in similar circumstances. One woman still couldn't find her children. She had two little girls who were taken from her when they were babies. They were teenagers now, but she had no idea where they were. The Embassy said her husband moved away, and they didn't know where he went with the children.

I talked to a man who said he would get the children for fifty-thousand dollars, but there was no guarantee that he would get them for sure. He said things can go wrong, and people have gotten killed for kidnapping children in Saudi Arabia.

He said they chop your head off. "So I've heard," I told him.

I also talked to a Saudi lawyer who said that I could go to court, but they wouldn't give me the children. Women don't have any rights under the Saudi law, especially since I'm American. The lawyer said chances are I would also be put in jail. "For what reason?" I asked. He said that I was an American. They think we are all caphers (Atheists). So I said, "I would never win?" He replied, "No, you will never win".

I decided that I would travel through the desert when my mom told me, "What would be the point of it if you were killed? The children will most likely come back to the United States when they're older. This is not the only part of their life. They are going to grow up, and they'll still need you when they are older. If you get yourself killed they will never, ever have you again. Even if you are not there with them now, they know where you are and that you still love them." I thought about it, and put it in God's hands.

My next decision was to go to a court of law in Indiana to get custody of all three of my children. With the assistance of a good attorney, I finally did win that battle. By the law of the United States I now have total custody of all three of my children even though the laws of Saudi Arabia won't recognize that. I grasped the legal documents in my hand knowing that this piece of paper wouldn't bring my children back to me either.

I was glad that I made sure that when they were born, they all three were registered as American citizens. This makes it legal for them to always be able to come home to America. This was my only hope for them to get back to me someday when they become older.

43. Tim and My New Life

I told Tim that I didn't know how I could go through another day without my children. I told him that I would need a baby just to want to go on in this life. He responded that would be okay with him when the time was right.

In the meantime, Tim tried his best to keep my mind off of the trauma that I had gone through. He took me to a wedding one night, and I found out that he was one of the best dancers that I had ever met. After the wedding he took me to the Patoka River in our hometown. It was a full moon, and I could tell the river was high after all the rain we had. The current was unusually strong. There was plenty of light from the moon and the light from the bridge above to see the foam on the white caps forming. They came gushing down the river hitting the sides of the bank. It suddenly reminded me of when my uncle Bud had tragically drowned in a river when trying to cross to the other side. At the point where we were standing huge rocks covered the banks which also led into the middle of the river. Tim of course was eagerly waiting to cross the rocks and coaxed me into following. He crossed over the rocks first, but kept his boots on. I took my shoes off only to feel the wet, slimy, slippery rocks beneath me. The next thing I knew I lost my balance and began falling backwards, but Tim put his steady arm out just in time to catch me. Amused by my clumsiness, he ordered me to hold onto his hand. We slowly crept out onto the rocks, and he put his arms around me as we squatted down to where the waves came gushing by. I was surprised that we weren't getting wet. It felt like the mist that came down in a rainforest as one is walking through at the zoo. It was scary to hear the thunderous sound of the river but beautiful at the same time with the full moon glistening on the water. It was paradise to me after living in the desert for so long. I wasn't afraid as I held Tim's hand, and I looked into his green eyes. I had a strange feeling that I was going to end up being with this crazy guy for the rest of my life. As we were in our own little world watching the waves go by something big, black, and furry jumped on the rock in front of us. I gasped, stood up and quickly started to crawl back to the bank as fast as could over the slimy rocks. "What was that," I said? Tim said that was the biggest muskrat that he had ever seen, but he wasn't sure that's what it was. Later on he came to find out that it was an otter.

I immediately decided to go back to college to get my bachelor's degree in Elementary Education. After teaching children in the Middle East for more than eight years, I knew that I wanted to continue teaching children and help them learn. This was one of the hardest and saddest times of my life. However, I knew this would be the only way to keep my sanity.

I also worked two nights a week teaching English to Spanish students which I enjoyed very much. Keeping busy with school and teaching nights did keep my mind occupied. There were days when I didn't want to go on without my children and didn't see much of a point of going on, but Tim always tried to keep me busy which helped my mind from wandering. I also found it hard to believe that I was only two minutes away from where I grew up as a little girl.

My dad stopped by one day to visit. He was probably worried about me as usual. When he walked in the house he gave me that funny look like something was wrong. I said, "Now what did I do?" He continued walking into the kitchen and asked if I had a towel. Puzzled, I handed him a kitchen towel. Then he walked back to the door that he came in and stuffed the towel in the doorknob hole. "Oh that, I said." "Tim just went to get a new doorknob so the hole in the door won't be there too long." Dad said, "You know, snakes can crawl in through that hole in the door." I never thought about that. As I recall when I was little there were an awful lot of black snakes around. That got me a bit worried. Amused, Dad said, "Maybe the towel will help for awhile."

My dad thought that it was incredibly ironic to end up where I was after living on the other side of the world for so long. I drove past my old home by the lake everyday, and I would always take a glance at the lake and my old house. It made me wonder how this all could have happened? Was it written or was it fate?

It was different looking at Tim everyday who has green eyes, sandy brown hair and a white complexion. He had a nice tan from the summer. Tim was forty-four when we first met. He had a tremendous amount of self-confidence and a lot of creative talent which I noticed when I first met him. He was also a great businessman and could carry a conversation with a trash can. He didn't seem to be afraid of much of anything. It also amazed me how strong he was when one day he was showing off and picked up the back of a car. I felt sorry for anybody that would try to pick a fight with him.

One summer when I went outside to get some tomatoes from our garden he was teasing a black snake with a stick near the garden. I, of course told him to kill it, screamed and ran away. He didn't kill it. I decided to let him pick the tomatoes that night. He didn't like to kill anything, unlike Mubarak. When Tim would catch a fish he would throw it back in the lake unless I told him that I wanted to eat it.

We were both completely different from each other as I liked anything to do with education or reading books, and he liked anything to do with cars, which was his career since he owned and operated his own body shop. I found out that he raced cars when he was younger and still has his race car in the back of his shop.

Fall was coming so Tim and I would rake leaves together. It was amazing to see leaves again and to smell them. I had forgotten so much what the life was like here. It was strange to be able to walk outside without covering my body with the black cape. I could open the door and walk outside in the yard wearing a tank top and shorts and not be afraid that I would be harassed, killed, or put in jail.

I was excited about Halloween coming. I found that I had met the right person for Halloween time. Tim was very much into all the holidays but especially Halloween. We went pumpkin hunting, and he ended up buying seventy-five pumpkins. We carved about twenty-pumpkins ourselves and took the rest to the local Moose club to give the rest to children to carve. We also dressed up in costumes and went to a Halloween party where there was turtle soup, fried turtle, fried chicken, and homemade French fries among other foods as well. There was also a hay ride which I hadn't done in years. It was good to be home again to enjoy the different seasons and holidays again.

Unfortunately, Mubarak kept calling during this time, which was torture to my mind. He kept repeating that the cards were in his hands. Furthermore, he wouldn't let me talk to the children. He said that he was remarried to a Saudi woman, which was what his family wanted him to do in the first place.

One time he called and said that Sarah had been hit by a car. That threw my mind for a loop. Mubarak said that she will probably have a limp for the rest of her life. Sometimes I wonder if she's even alive because no one will let me talk to her. She was two years old the last time I saw her face or talked to her.

Just when I was at the end of my rope and didn't know how to go on living my life without a child, Tim suddenly proposed to me. On Christmas Eve of 2000 he told me to stand by our huge seventeen foot, decorated, and all lit-up Christmas tree. He got down on his knees and proposed. I said yes, and he gave me a beautiful gold diamond ring.

The following week, I went to the doctor and found out that I was pregnant. Well, if nothing else Tim had good timing for proposing. He, of course, wanted to get married right away, but I knew that I had to finish college first. We waited until I got my bachelor's degree. I could only hope that God would forgive me for not getting married immediately.

When I was pregnant Tim kept getting phone calls from Mubarak. Mubarak kept threatening to kill him. He said that he was going to send an Arab who was living in the states to kill him and blow up his home. I figured he was bluffing, but Tim got fed up and finally called the FBI and told them what was going on. We gave them as much information as we could about Mubarak. They said they would try to find out if there was somebody close by who could harm us. We didn't hear from the FBI agent again, and the phone calls from Mubarak stopped for awhile. Tim was on edge knowing that we were going to have a baby, and we kept getting death threats. He decided to keep his guns loaded and close by just in case. I wondered why Mubarak did this when he said that he had married an Arabic woman and already had a baby from her. He needed to concentrate on his family at this time not us.

I kept getting fatter with the baby on the way and was hoping that nothing drastic was going to happen since it was getting close to my delivery date which was supposed to be September 15. Ironically, I started my labor on the morning of the terrorist attack of September 11, 2001. I woke up with pains and was trying to rest just in case this was going to be the day, when suddenly the phone rang. I was having a bad feeling again like something else was going to happen and then the phone rang. It startled me for some reason and I almost fell out of bed. I answered the phone. It was Tim, who was in town doing some work. He told me to turn the television on because there had been an attack on the United States in New York. I said, "No way." He said I should turn the television on right now. I said okay and told him that I was just starting my contractions. Then he said, "No way." I replied, "I am." He told me to watch what was happening on CNN and said that he would call me back in a bit to see how I was doing. I couldn't believe this was happening. The Arabs again, and I was having a baby. Why was this happening? I saw a plane hit the twin towers. It was like watching a movie. Tim called back and said they hit the Pentagon, and The White House might be their next target. He said that he was going to fill up the car with gas because everybody in town was getting worried about what was going on. He said there were people lined up everywhere filling up their gas tanks. I nervously replied, "Okay, but don't forget to come home because this baby is coming no matter what the terrorists blow up." He asked how far apart my contractions were, and I said about fifteen minutes right now. He said that he would be home soon, but somehow I doubted that. I decided to try and get some rest because this was not going to be a good thing, having a baby while there was a terrorist attack going on in the United States. All I kept thinking was that nobody was ever going to take this baby away from me.

We went to the hospital later on in the afternoon, but things didn't get going with the baby until about nine o'clock. The doctors, nurses and everybody were watching CNN. I was just hoping that our hospital wouldn't be bombed. Then what? Were the sirens going to go off as soon as I was going to have a baby? Would everybody run and leave me alone? I thought to myself that must be paranoid. Here I am back home again trying to start my life over having a baby, and I'm still having to worry about the Arabs. Well, at least we weren't in Washington D.C.

I was praying that the baby would be born on September 12 and not today, the 11th. She had three more hours to hold off, which she did. Samantha was born at two in the morning. She waited too long as far as I was concerned. My husband was about to pass out at the end because she came out blue as can be, but after the doctor smacked her little butt, she screamed and started looking better. My mom and Tim went home almost immediately. They both looked exhausted, and they didn't even have to do anything. I just thanked God for letting me have this baby. I looked at her and knew that I was going to spoil her terribly after losing my other children, but that would be okay with me.

The next summer I graduated from college with a bachelor's degree in Elementary Education. Shortly after that Tim and I got married. Tim, his friends and I cooked all the food for the wedding. That was a lot of work— cooking for almost four hundred people. I couldn't believe that I was going to have a wedding after never being able to have one before. I was thirty-six years old now. After thirty-six years, my name was going to change, too. I had always kept my maiden name all of my life because the Arabs don't let their wives carry their names. I was finally happy again having my little girl and my American husband.

We were married on November 16th, in a small church. It snowed as we left the church. I thanked God for all the friends and family that he had blessed me with. But somehow I still didn't feel totally complete. I often wondered what that feeling was, but I knew down in my heart as long as I live that I would never feel complete without my three children. I did know that life had to go on, and people would have to stop asking me about my children in the Middle East when it was completely out of my hands. There is nothing else that I can do but wait. I wondered at times how people can be so cruel. They always ask the same thing when they see me, and then they just walk away without even asking how I am or talking about anything else. Maybe they didn't know they were hurting me, or did they? I prayed for what to do. Should I leave my hometown? Was it time to completely disappear again and go to somewhere like Alaska? How ironic for me to think about going to Alaska after living in the desert for almost fourteen years. Of course, I overcame those thoughts and decided to stay because I knew Tim wouldn't move away. I would just have to walk away from the people who seemed to want to hurt me or to me it seemed that way. In time things changed and I became stronger. I became less sensitive and learned how to deal with the situation and people's comments which were less frequent.

I also came to a realization that in this small town it was going to be next to impossible to get a teaching position. Nobody was retiring or the schools would just shuffle previously employed teachers around the school system. My professors told me to move to Nevada, Florida, or North Carolina, but I couldn't leave Tim. He took care of me and supported me while I went back to school to get my education, even though I guess I won't ever be able to use it here. I had so much experience in teaching and education, but I didn't know what to do. My mom kept telling me to stay positive, things will open up, and many teachers will be retiring in a few years. I was getting tired of people asking me if I had gotten a teaching job. They wouldn't say hi to me or ask how I am only, "Did you get a teaching position yet?" Then they would walk away and not talk to me again. I wondered if it would ever end. Would I even have the courage to go on this time? Did my Indonesian maid in Saudi Arabia put such strong black magic that I would have to suffer for the rest of my life looking for happiness? Mubarak said that the spell she put on me was very strong and may never go away. I had so much faith in God all my life to carry me through so many traumatic ordeals that I couldn't make myself believe that was true. I was just having a streak of bad luck and maybe I was supposed to be doing something else, but I was finally getting tired.

Tim and I shortly before our engagement

Tim, me, and Samantha

44. The Accident

U ndaunted by my bad luck, I decided to take a drive to where my mamaw and papaw lived in a small town not very far away. I went into a school and talked to the principal. He told me that he had a part-time position, but that I would have to go back to school for special training. I didn't feel that I could do that with Samantha still not in school, but later on I did take a position there only to lose that, too after hitting a semi- truck on the way home from school. It was a bad crash, and the man driving the chicken truck said I was lucky to be alive from what I overheard from my husband later on. None of the chickens were injured like I was.

For some reason right before impact I checked my seat belt which was loose. I tightened it and soon after, my van hit the semi and flipped around in circles. I had a strange feeling that I might die, but I wasn't afraid. I only prayed for my family to be strong if I die and for Samantha and my children to be well taken care of. Maybe my faith in God was stronger than I thought. I dove straight down about ten or more feet into an embankment. My face came to an inch of touching the windshield even with my seatbelt on. As the car kept flipping around in circles, I asked God to let the car stop and let the engine die because as I looked behind me, there was another drop that went into a deep stream. As soon as I asked God to make the car to stop, it did and right then and there with a fog of smoke covering the van. I couldn't feel my left leg and knew something was wrong. I pushed the door open, but was dizzy and thought I had better sit. I presumed that my leg was broken from such a hard impact. Some men out of nowhere came running and helped me. They told me not to get out and one man got in the van and braced my neck and said to stay still until the ambulance came. Soon the ambulance arrived and took me to the hospital. I had broken my leg in three places and my ribs were bruised. I was having a hard time breathing as well and guessed it was from the seatbelt as I saw the black and blue line across my chest from where the seatbelt had been.

After six months and several weeks of physical therapy, I was still using a cane. The therapist said that there was a young man who was coming for therapy with the same break as I and was still using a cane after two years. She said that I would be lucky if I would ever walk normally again. Fortunately, my dad, who was now retired, made sure that I continued physical therapy as needed. After my dad saw my x-rays he told me that I had better never get crazy and be jumping off any tables because he said that my leg would break in half because one bone in my leg was hanging that looked really crushed.

Why was this happening again? Why did I have to keep starting from the bottom and never make a normal life work? Or was this just the way my life was going to be, having one traumatic experience after another with no end to it all? I know now if it weren't for my dad pushing me to walk, I would not have gone to therapy. He also shook his head and said the harder that I work or try at something the worse things get for me. He said that I was a good girl, and he would never understand it. Both my parents taught me perseverance, and that helped me get through a lot of the situations I got myself into. Mom always would tell us, "The Holland girls don't give up." "We are not quitters!" I've been wondering about that these past few days. My daughter, Samantha who is now in the first grade recently said, "Mom if you give up then you failed," "Don't ever give up!" I really cried after she said that. My sister Lisa tells her four children the same thing. "We are not quitters."

I did start walking again, but it was slow. I have to wear good, supportive shoes if I go fishing with Tim and Samantha or go on short walks with my mom. Tim doesn't understand, but that's one reason why I don't take as many long walks with him as I used to.

I kept on having thoughts that I would never have my own classroom as a teacher in my hometown. Maybe I wasn't pushing hard enough. It didn't seem to be in the cards right now, here in my hometown. How sad I thought. Was my life always going to be this way constantly continuing to struggle for a better life that will never come? Was it written this way before I was born, and I can't change the outcome no matter how hard I try? Is that why sometimes we feel that we have already been to that place before? Were our lives truly written to be like a movie that can't be stopped or changed? This would be interesting to do some research on-not that anybody hasn't tried to already to no avail, but I wonder.

As I reflected on the situation, I decided to stay positive. "Ah, I have an idea. This is a good time to start writing a book." What other back up plan did I have except to possibly be a belly dancer? I told my mom my back up plan, and she gave me that stern look and said that it's not funny. I told her that I was joking. It was fun to see what kind of response I might get from her.

Maybe it was written as the Arabs say that I was to write this book and never teach again. The culture and religion of Arabia would never leave my thoughts as long as I live, but Samantha's thoughts were in my mind as well. "Don't ever give up on your dreams, Mom!"

45. Dad

The following year my dad became ill with congestive heart failure. I was content that I had time to spend with him while mom continued to work part-time. My mom and he asked for me to stay with him instead of having strangers take care of him while mom worked during the day. She later told me that this may have been a blessing in disguise (that I didn't have a full time job yet) and would give me time with him that I had missed for so many years. Toward the end he was very weak and told me how it was funny that he used to take care of me, and now I was taking care of him. In the last days before he died, it really made me think about life and how precious it is. He grabbed my hand one day and said that he knew he was dying and told me to promise him that I would enjoy life. He told me to take time to have fun, laugh, and do as much as I could because time is too short on this earth. I teased him and said that maybe I should be a black jack dealer at the famous hotel resort nearby. He told me to cut it out and that I should stick to my dream. I was getting tired of that dumb dream that wasn't working out. I wanted to laugh again and my dream wasn't making me happy anymore.

He became very sick that day. I would hold his head up while he got sick and vomited in a bowl. He couldn't even eat the jello that I made for him. I put wet cloths on his head and propped his legs up when his legs would fill up with fluid. He had been in and out of the hospital for months, but I knew this was the last time. He told me that he couldn't stand the pain anymore and needed to get back to the hospital.

The next morning I went to the hospital to stay with dad for awhile. There seemed to be a lot of commotion going on as I walked down the hall. My oldest sister walked out of my dad's room and then I saw an angry looking nurse walking directly toward me and asked, " Who are you, and who is that tall woman in the purple blouse?" I told her that was my oldest sister, and I was the youngest daughter. She said that I could go in, but that my dad was very upset after my sister had visited, and they didn't want that one to come back in the room. I went into the room only to see my dad huffing and puffing and growling. He looked like he wanted to kill somebody. I hadn't seen that look since I broke my curfew when I was a senior in high school, and he took my car keys away. I told him that maybe he should sit down and asked him what's wrong? He was so angry that he was getting himself wrapped up in his oxygen cord. I thought that I better unwind the cord before he strangled himself and then got him to sit down. I asked if he wanted me to leave. I could come back later.

He said no, that he wanted me to stay, that it was the other one he was mad at. I figured my oldest sister was annoying him again. She was being good at that lately, and mom and I couldn't figure out what was happening with her. He got sick again and lay back on the bed. Suddenly his body flew forward which scared me to death. He looked at me and asked what happened. I presumed that his defibrillator had just gone off. I called for the nurse, and she confirmed that it just went off. He was sleeping peacefully now. The nurse said whoever the woman was in the purple shirt really upset him. Then my sister Lisa from Maryland called and asked what was going on? She said that the nurse kept asking her who the woman in the purple shirt was as well. I told her what happened and told her that she could talk to dad if she wanted. He seemed a bit more rested right now.

Mom was in New York evaluating a college education program and flew home early when I called and told her dad was sick again. He did recover some, but the doctors told her about a month later, she had better get the daughter living in Maryland home.

I was relieved when my sister Lisa and her four children made it home from Maryland to see dad. I was thankful that she got to talk to him before he was finally put on morphine. He died about a week after she arrived. The night he died, my mom and I were talking about my son Khalid and were hoping that maybe he would be coming to visit us soon. My dad seemed to be trying to talk and moved his fingers. My mom said, "I think he hears us talking about Kelly." Dad always called Khalid, Kelly.

My sister Lisa, and her four children, and Samantha and I went to Mom's house so we could all be together for the night. When the phone rang at eight' o clock, we looked at each other and knew that he had died. Lisa picked up the phone. It was our oldest sister. (She had gone to the hospital and stayed with mom shortly before he died.) She said that dad had died. Moments later, mom called as well. How hard it is when one's father dies. That night my sister said she could smell dad's smoke from his pipe in the house. I kept hearing and seeing things as well. In the morning we both said the way he was always playing tricks on everybody you can never tell. Maybe it really was him floating around at night.

After my dad died our oldest sister and her family left the state of Indiana, and we haven't heard from her since. My mom and my sister, Lisa, said that was like having three deaths in the family at once. (My oldest sister had a little boy Samantha's age, and he was gone too.) Our oldest sister had a falling out with my dad right before he died. The whole family was pretty stressed out during the ordeal and following dad's death.

Dad and Khalid, the Christmas I went home

46. Khalid Comes to America

How strange that a few weeks after my dad died, my son Khalid came home. My dad always talked about Kelly and how he wanted to see his grandson again. How sad that dad wasn't going to see him now that he was all grown up. Khalid was soon to be eighteen, and he would be here on his birthday.

Khalid called from Saudi Arabia one day and said that he wanted to come see me. He was also thinking about attending college at a University in Indiana.

(My mom had been emailing him for a couple of years about going to college in America.) I was wondering what he looked like now, and if I would recognize him when we went to pick him up at the airport. It had been about eight years since I had seen him. I told Samantha that her brother was coming to visit us from Saudi Arabia and of course, she had a hard time understanding where Saudi Arabia was; but, she was excited that she was going to see her brother after looking at his pictures when he was little. I told her that he is a lot older now. Being a five year old she was always in her own little world, so who knows what she was thinking. I just hoped that she would be able to get along with him.

Tim kept pacing back and forth at the airport while Samantha followed two steps behind him. I sat down in a chair by the airport windows and waited anxiously. I wondered what he would be like and would he still be my little Khalid that I knew. His plane finally arrived.

215

I told Tim that I was afraid I wouldn't know who he was, but Tim said that I would. Then I saw him and knew who he was right away. He still had his baby face and features that I recognized. He was taller than me with broad shoulders and the beautiful olive skin and the dark brown eyes and dark brown hair. We hugged and started talking just like we had never been apart.

When we got home we continued talking. He talked about school and was very happy that he graduated from high school in the spring. The students in Saudi Arabia only have three years of high school, so he was seventeen when he finished. He was still so young. He reminded me of myself at his age. All I wanted to do was travel around the world. I could tell that he had that in him, too. My mother's instinct was telling me that he might not have come here just to go to college. I think he wanted to see me, but he had something else up his sleeve as well.

We talked very late. Samantha who continued eavesdropping on our conversation not wanting to miss anything, finally decided to go to bed. She was hanging and jumping all over Kelly and would just stare at him. She asked why he talked funny and was that English. I explained to her that he had an Arabic accent because he lived in a far away country called Saudi Arabia. I told her she might hear him speak Arabic to me as well. She had a hard time even pronouncing the word Arabic.

Khalid said that Nadia and Sarah were doing well. Nadia loved to study and go to school. It sounded like she was a very good cook, too. Her favorite show was Oprah Winfrey and wished that one day she could meet her. He said she would watch it everyday and no one was allowed to turn the channel when Oprah came on. She was hoping to study to be a journalist after she graduated from high school. I was glad to hear she was thinking about her future and hoped that she could come see me someday, too.

Khalid told me not to cry because he would get her out of Saudi Arabia so she could see me again. He said that he didn't think his dad would ever let Sarah out of Saudi. He started talking about his grandma and told me that she had used black magic on me so that I would leave his dad. He said that she had it planned for a long time. Evidently she wanted Mubarak to marry an Arabian woman which was no surprise to me. He said that his dad had remarried and had two children, but Khalid didn't seem to want to talk about his stepmother. He would cleverly change the subject.

The next day I took Khalid to enroll in a university that was about ten minutes from my home. After three weeks he decided that he wanted to go to New York to go to school. He said that he didn't feel like he fit in this small town where we lived. He said that the people always stare at him and probably think that he's a terrorist. I told him that I doubt that, but I knew he wasn't very happy.

One of his uncles was living in New York, so I called him and he said that Khalid could come and live with him and go to college in New York. I couldn't believe that he would be leaving me again, but I realized that he was about to turn eighteen and wanted to travel and be on his own. I was remembering how I was at that age. My mom and dad had a lot of patience with me, and now I have to have patience with my own children. "What goes around comes around," my dad always said. I asked him to try to finish college for a year, but he insisted on going to New York. I decided to let him try it since I knew that family was there.

I cried again when he left and knew that he would never really be mine again. He wanted to be in his own world with his own people, just like I wanted to be when I left Saudi Arabia. He seemed to be more Arabian than Americanized. Sadly enough, he had forgotten most of what I had taught him.

Khalid called about everyday for awhile and talked to me. It was nice to be able to talk to him so much after not being able to for so long. I didn't like the idea that he was in New York. I knew what it was like there because I had visited a friend there and felt overwhelmed with the vastness of that city. It was okay if you had a plan though and knew what you wanted to do, but I knew my son didn't have much of a plan going on after talking to him. He told me later that he went to school for awhile but decided to work somewhere instead and help his uncle pay the rent. I had a feeling he might not be staying there too long either. After a couple of months he said that his uncle was thinking about moving back to Saudi Arabia, so Khalid said that he was thinking to move back as well.

Before he left for Saudi Arabia he came back to see me. He said that he was thinking about going to college at a school in Egypt or maybe Malaysia. It sounded like he wanted to travel a bit and wasn't quite sure what to do. I told him that I loved him no matter where he was or what he did. After two weeks he left again.

It was very hard for me after he left. I wondered if that was it, and I would never see him again. I wondered if I should have made him stay with me. How could I have kept him against his own free will? He was a young man who wanted to see the world. He said that he missed his sisters and his friends. I couldn't blame him for that. He had his life in Saudi Arabia, and I had my new life in the United States. I was just having a hard time dealing with it. How did all of this happen anyway? Sometimes I wondered where God was and why wasn't he ever coming through for me? Why did I have to lose all of my children? What was the purpose or the reason of it in this life? I went to hug Samantha and told her that I loved her. I knew that I would unduly spoil Samantha after losing my other children. I do thank God for Samantha everyday that I wake up.

I don't hear from Khalid very often. The last time I talked to him he was attending college for business in Riyadh, Saudi Arabia. He said that he liked it there and said that he was thinking about bringing Nadia home with him in the summer to visit. I talked to Nadia recently and she said, "I want to see my momma, It's not right that I can't see you. It has been too long and baba (dad) needs to let me come and see you." I was about to cry and told her that I will see her again. I talked to her in Arabic. I thought it might be easier for her if I did. She didn't know that I could speak so well. She asked me how I knew how to speak Arabic. I told her that I had lived in the Middle East for almost fourteen years and had taught myself how to speak the language. I explained to that she was too young at the time to understand that I talked to her in English and Arabic. It made me realize how little she knew about me, but I doubted if Mubarak had told her anything good about me, or for that matter, anything at all. Even though mom keeps encouraging me to communicate with the children, I find it very hard to talk to Khalid and Nadia on the phone when I can't see them in person. It has become harder and harder through the years. I thought it would become easier, but it has become worse for me to decide what to do about it. I only hope to see them again and realize that I can never change the past. Many times I wonder how my life would have turned out if I had crossed through the desert in Jordon to try to get the children. I guess I'll never know, but at that time after losing everything that I owned I didn't have the finances nor could I find anyone who wanted to risk their lives to go through such treacherous conditions. My last attempt was when I went to Amsterdam and after that nightmare I decided that it was time to stay put in my own country. I'm lucky that I still have my mom who has always stood by me no matter how bad things have gotten for me.

Tim, me, Khalid, and Samantha

47. The End

I still pray today for guidance or an answer to what happened. It has become hard at times to find the strength to want to get up in the morning to face another day without my three beautiful children, but then Samantha with her mischievous smiling face, giggles and then jumps on the bed and me. Then I know I have to keep going and try to live my life to the fullest because of her and my husband Tim, who at times probably thinks I still look lost just like when he first met me, and I walked into his house with nothing but the clothes on my back.

The problem is that sometimes I still get that "lost" feeling and wonder if I'm half Arabian as well as American. The culture of Arabia is so ancient and incredibly strong that once a person lives there for a long period of time, you can never forget it. I know that I never will forget some of the wonderful people whom I met there and their culture as well as the religion.

I realize now that my future is what I make it. I must be positive, go forward, and let the past rest. I will.

My dad was right though, it is not always better on the other side.

Samantha-The ice storm

hi mom I hop To Syw Soon
I loVEy very mach I looooooVEy
and Sam anTha and grand mother
mom I weuT To Seuw ples I went
To Touke weTh you and laf weTh
you and do evEry Theng To gTher
I hop To Com AmeruKa inThe
Summey To Seaw how is
Ariaebg weTh you do you
Lrend faster bKoos naw
I lrend Englich it is To
haved I hopThe geeFT it
Laky.

A letter from my daughter

I well seuw son
ok mom I LoVEy so so
sooooooo mach pleis can
you LoVEy I an jo ken weth
you I looooooooooooooooo ooo

VEy
your &ofev:·
Nadia

E meil
No No_ fm @ maKTooB.Con.

Made in the USA
Lexington, KY
19 June 2018